Permission to Be YOU

Personal Insignificance to Workplace Magnificence

Jivi Saran

Permission to Be YOU

First Published in Canada 2016 by The Corporate Mentalist Inc.

Copyright © 2016 by Jivi Saran
All rights reserved. No part of this publication may be reproduced, stored in or introduced into a retrieval system, or transmitted, in any form, or by any means (electronic, mechanical, photocopying, recording or otherwise) without the prior written permission of the publisher. This book is sold subject to the condition that it shall not, by way of trade or otherwise, be lent, resold, hired out, or otherwise circulated without the publisher's prior consent in any form of binding or cover other than that in which it is published and without a similar condition including this condition being imposed on the subsequent purchaser.

Book Cover Design: Kenneth Pugmire
Editor: Nina Shoroplova
Typeset: Greg Salisbury
Portrait Photographer: Craig Letourneau

DISCLAIMER: This book is a guide intended to offer information on how to connect with oneself and others. It is not intended in any way to replace other professional health care or mental health advice, but to support it. Readers of this publication agree that neither the author nor her publisher will be held responsible or liable for damages that may be alleged or resulting directly or indirectly from the reading of this publication

In dedication to the LightonLight family, non physical and physical. In the "star" I asked for courage, vitality and fluidity to be me and SO IT IS. Love beyond measure.

Testimonials

"Written with impeccable grace, love, and self-deprecating humility, Permission to Be You shares the life journey of one woman's human foibles, misconceptions, and heartrending challenges. Through the author's awe-inspiring courage and resilience, the reader vicariously experiences a true transformation as Jivi takes decisive action to reclaim her true life purpose. This true story inspires every person and every leader to recognize that we have the answers we seek and when we have the courage to listen to our inner voice and follow the wisdom of our being, we will find peace, happiness, and great personal freedom. Jivi, you are a beautiful soul, a wonderful woman, and I am blessed to have met and experienced your graciousness."
Shelley Rathie, CPHR, MBA, LLM, Mount Royal University, Bissett School of Business Faculty, Choosing Happiness, SAGE Advisor

"This book takes to the soul of a sage leader and guide. She has worn many costumes, unwanted and wanted, but always has had a sense that there was a wise and worthy soul to be fashioned beneath them all. This book shows you how you, too, can do that and take your unique brilliance into every one of your circles of influence."
Brian Fraser, Lead Provocateur, Jazzthink

"Jivi delivers a beautifully disruptive story packed with powerful exercises to help you unpack your own life and move forward as a veritable leader. Permission to Be You is a truly captivating and rewarding read."
Christine Gustafson, PEng, Principal at Harbourgreene Consulting Inc.

"What a terrific book. It is honest, vulnerable, and humorous. It is a roadmap for us to hear Jivi's brilliantly spun stories and see her truth, which makes it safe to see our own. Jivi gives permission for the reader to grow, remove their own costume through simple exercises, and to do it all without judgment. Highly recommend this book to anyone looking for a better way; a better version of themselves."
Alison Donaghey, author, speaker, thought strategist, dominothinking.com

"Jivi tells her own story so we can find the courage to examine ours and shed the weight of the invisible clothing that is holding us down, keeping us back. Her book wakes up the soul and lovingly challenges us and helps us to address the questions we've been hiding from: Who am I? How can I find the 'me' that's been buried under the weight of early experience and self-doubt? How can I work from acceptance to joy?"
Ann Perodeau, MA, Social Change Facilitator

"Jivi Cheema shares her inspiring story with courage and authenticity. This book is an invitation and a guide to soul searching and self empowerment. It should be included in any organisation's orientation package so that staff can learn about corporate mindfulness."
Seynabou Diack, Director, SMD Consulting Inc.

"Jivi's story moved and inspired me, to my core. She encourages us to live our life to the fullest by believing in our self and our ability to stay true and remain authentic."
Catherine Brownlee, Global Headhunter connecting people globally

"Jivi's relatable stories confirm our authentic selves are hiding in clear sight. This book is a guide to your 'BIG reveal.' Get ready! Jivi's decisions demonstrate that the 'Good Life' doesn't only happen for certain people—it's your choice! If you are reading this book, your heart knows it is time to change your story. Jivi's approach to change encourages you to tame your critic and be completely open with the only person who hears what is in your head and heart—you. This delightful read confirms that simple questions and gentle inquisition can have an enormous effect for you and your team!"
Jana De Luca

"Permission to Be You by Jivi Saran is a wonderful book everyone must read. She shares her life journey and shows how others can work on themselves to overcome challenges in a positive way."
Judy Magnussen

Acknowledgements

There are so many people who have come in and out of my life, not only while I was writing this book but also many of you may be a part of these stories and the reason that this book, Permission to Be You , is possible. Without these life experiences with you, there would have been no story for me to write. I realize I am seeing this through only one angle and no doubt you may recall some details being different, so I acknowledge that this is simply my side of the story and I am forever grateful to each of you for being a part of my life.

I am who I am today because of my tenacity, persistence, and resilience, which have come from how I saw my parents living their lives. I have gained my courage and fearlessness from my father and my bravery, peace, and drive for life from my mother. These characteristics combined have helped me deal with the obstacles and challenges that have come up in my life. As I was writing this book there were many times when I had to heal some parts of myself that were still hiding deep inside. Many times I would find myself pulling on courage, fearlessness, and bravery to put this story down on paper. I am forever grateful for the lessons my parents have taught me, because those very lessons have made me a better person.

My two children—Neena and Raj—have supported me through all the challenges that life circumstances have brought my way. Without them supporting me, guiding me, and being there each step of the way, I might not have written this book. When I see their optimistic approach to obstacles, their zest for life, and their motivation to be great people in the world, I am reminded of unconditional love. They are wise beyond their years, and the many conversations we have about life are often filled with wisdom, laughter, and compassion. Both my kids are precious in their own way and yet have the same outcome—unconditional love for me.

My sister Neeta, who went to the boarding school in India with me, has in all ways—personal, professional, and financial—supported me my entire life, whether she agreed with my life choices or not. She has given me the strength and courage to follow my dreams even if at times she thought I was crazy. She believed in me at the worst of times and the best of times, even when no one else did. Just when I think I can't love her or admire her any more, I am filled with even more love and admiration. My brother Cory helped me live out my dream of the television show and made possible something that I thought was impossible. His passion for family values and standing out as an individual is truly admirable. My younger sister, Joti, has taught me so much vicariously about standing up for what you believe in at all costs, and many a time, I have found myself thinking, "If only I had the same assertiveness she does and could say it with a like-it-is attitude." In all the good and the bad, the great challenges and the successes we have faced together and individually, we are still family, and for that I am truly grateful.

Ruby Bedi, my "Soul Caretaker," is my mentor, guide, coach, friend, and anything else that I need her to be on any given day. She has played so many roles in my life that it is difficult to count them. She is the gentle whisper that constantly reminds me of my soul journey and keeps me on track with my soul script. She is always encouraging me to be the best person I can be on any given day. She gently nudges me out of my comfort zone every day just far enough to keep me on my toes so that I am presenting my authentic self to the world. Her greatest gifts to me are to be a lightning rod for my soul and to then tell me, "Go sleep on it!"

My very close friend Heather has been a pillar of strength for me over the last decade. She has always been there for me even at the toughest times of her life. I admire her for her strength, love, and courage toward life; she is unstoppable at giving of herself to her friends and family. She has seen me at my worst and my best (okay, I'll admit maybe more often at my worst) and she loves me unconditionally just the same. When I look back at the toughest times of my life, I knew I could always count on you to be there by my side, in person or in spirit. For you, dear friend, I am grateful.

Margaret Connelly, Janine Karlsen, Nick Baldwin, Jeremy Smith—each of you has been a key milestone in my thirty-year career, a milestone whom I will forever cherish. My career literally was not possible had each one of you not believed in me and had faith in my gifts to the business world. Margaret, from you I learned business acumen and management. Janine, from you I learned how leadership can be compassionate and nurturing. Nick, from you I have learned the value of co-leadership, that when two diverse people with opposite strengths come together with similar foundational values, high team-performance magic happens, and for this I am grateful to you. You, Jeremy, allowed me the greatest gift of all: you gave me permission to bring all my learning together and be my authentic self in the workplace. You valued my whole being, the good, the bad, and sometimes the ugly, regardless of what I was going through in my personal life and expected me to be the best that I could be on each given day. You pushed me beyond my comfort zone and allowed me to practice what I knew inside my heart to be the right thing to do in leadership. Working with you has set the foundation for my life's work around creating happier workplaces because we proved it worked under your leadership. I will always hold up all four of you as examples of leadership whom I admire.

MamaG, you have been the epitome of pure love and transformation in my life. You have shown me that loves exists in everything and that we don't need to go searching past ourselves to shine in that love. At a time when I felt most fragmented from love and relationships, you showed me a different path, one of self-love and self-forgiveness. The light that shines inside me and gives me permission to be myself comes from the light of love within you. One day, under your wing, I asked for strength, vitality, and fluidity for the work I was going to begin on this book, and here I stand now, my raw authentic self on paper. I love you, indeed!

Even while I was writing this book, many other friends encouraged me, inspired me, and kept me motivated to continue to heal. Each in their own way contributed to "Project Jivi." To you I am thankful for the roles you play in my life—Maggie, Lori, Judy, Kavita, Andrea, Ronna, Isaiaha, Dawn, Alison, Jana, Seynabou, and many others. Thank you!

Thank you, Sheila Kennedy, for helping me bring this book to the world. It has been such a pleasure working with you. I look forward to a long friendship going forward. Your passion for marketing is a truly remarkable, heart-centered gift that you bring to the world. Thank you.

William Oliver, Shine Kelly, and Kenneth Pugmire, thank you for all of your support in developing my business in a way that I never thought possible. You have taken me to a new platform and I could not have asked for a better team to make the magic happen. I attribute the amazing growth we have experienced in the last year to you.

Acknowledgements

Julie Salisbury, what can I even say? You are the most magnificent person and I am truly blessed to have met you. You made the process of publishing this book so easy. You were always there to guide, support, and inspire me to get this story on paper. You believed in and nurtured the storyteller in me, for which I thank you and your team for making this book a reality for me.

To everyone reading this book I offer my heartfelt gratitude that you have chosen to spend time reading about my journey. Your journey begins here, now.

Contents

Acknowledgements IX

Introduction 1

Chapter 1: Not Wanting to Turn On the Lights 7
Chapter 2: Shackled by Limiting Beliefs 21
Chapter 3: Paralyzed by Life Choices 31
Chapter 4: Deep Yearning to Be Different but Not Knowing How 47
Chapter 5: Blame Others for the Circumstances of Our Reality 71
Chapter 6: Look at Life as a Series of Seemingly Unrelated Events 93
Chapter 7: Not Willing to Go through the Pain of Healing 109
Chapter 8: Whole People 129
Chapter 9: Tired of Wearing a Costume for Society 151
Chapter 10: Bringing It All Together through "Project Jivi" 171

Epilogue 195
Author Biography 199
About Jivi 200

Exercises

Mind Mapping 18
Lights On 19
Breaking Free 30
Problem Paralysis 45

XV

Small Shifts Create Big Impact	68
How to Move from Your Reality to What You Desire	70
Holding Up the Mirror	91
Finding the Overlapping Patterns	107
Five Crucial Steps in the Spiritual and Emotional Self-Healing Process	126
Suffering Be Gone	128
Factors for Creating a Safe Environment at Work	146
Removing the Quilt	170
Identifying Your Support Team	192

Introduction

As the world sleeps in the quiet embrace of the darkness of the night, I sit here listening to the soft whispers of my soul guiding me to complete this book. The voice of my soul becomes clearer and listening becomes easier now that I wear no costume. As it is three in the morning, there is not a sound either in the house or outside; in this silence my soul's voice is loud and clear without any distractions.

Believe me when I say that if you had said to me five years ago, "Jivi, you will write a book describing the impact of the events of your life experiences," I would have laughed at you and probably responded with, "You've got to be joking. I would never disclose my personal story, and what does that even have to do with work? And who would want to read that!" Not in my wildest dreams would I have ever thought I would write a book that would talk openly about who I am behind closed doors. I would never have thought I would bring together the vulnerability of my life lessons with the work environment so that other people could be inspired to be themselves.

The last six years of contemplation and reflection of my life are almost as though I was reciting someone else's story through a movie and I am simply a character in each segment of the movie. This book brings all of my learning together by my reflecting on everything that has transpired in my life.

Hopefully, I will show you that absolute stunning beauty can arise from the ashes of the costume you have been wearing. It is the beauty of your authentic self and who you were always meant to be. If you are reading this book, give yourself permission today to be YOU as you read through my journey of becoming ME.

You may have forgotten the person who sits inside of you yearning to come out and be heard. You know that person so intimately, you can even hear and feel her from time to time. It's the voice you sometimes make quiet, because there is so much to get done and you can't really think about yourself right now.

There are probably many other people and things going on in your life. You ask how you can be so selfish as to think about yourself. You may have kids who depend on you, maybe a spouse to take care of; you may be a caregiver to someone special; and let's not forget work and all the things going on at work and all the people who need you to be there for them. How can you just put all this off and think about yourself? "There are only so many hours in a day and I am lucky if I have time to go to the washroom."

Do any of these thoughts sound familiar? They sound very familiar to me. I lived by them for years, believing them to be my reality. Putting myself last and everyone else before me, everything and everyone else took priority over me. Everything else was more important and even more critical than I was.

Today, I ask you, "When will you take on the project of YOU?"

Being on this earth among seven billion people, realize that no one else has exactly the same genetic makeup as you. What does that say to you? Would it not mean that you are here to contribute to this earth in a magnificent way? In a way that calls to your soul and makes your heart sing? Once I decided to remove my costume of all the things that I thought made me who I was, I found myself standing there in a place of transformation, in a place from which anything was possible, and in a place where only I was making decisions for my life.

I have learned that the life for each of us is exactly as we choose to make it and that each moment is divinely guided to be exactly as it should be for our soul script. My journey is one in which I traveled from feeling insignificant, without any choices, to feeling pure magnificence within myself.

I have written this book as an account of my life and how I showed up to work so that you get an in-depth realization that each member of your team has a story that they are going through, whether they tell it to you or not. The next time you look around your boardroom table, imagine each person sitting there wearing a costume of all the stories they think to be true about themselves—and don't leave yourself out, because you may be in the same canoe. It's now time to accept the whole person into the workplace so that we are not living the life of a lie and so we can be authentic about who we are in each moment.

In my life I have done a lot of self-healing, and simultaneously I have had a team of people that, over a six-year period, was able to pilot all the methodologies that I teach with magnificent results with lasting impact. I was speaking to a past team member recently and she said, "You really screwed us for life to work in any other environment."

I was shocked and asked, "Why?"

She responded, "You treated us like human beings first and team members after. We knew we could approach the leadership team with anything and we would not be judged for it. You created an environment in which we felt loved and cared for as people."

The word "love" really hits home for me. We shy away from this word in organizations, often thinking it's a taboo word that may cause some sort of disrespectful workplace. Yet, there can be organizational love from the perspective of respect and kindness to each person who is just trying to continue their own journey as they know best. It's time that we as leaders recognize and accept that we are dealing with the full story of the people on our teams, whether or not we see the full story externally. We need to help our team members take off their costumes. Without taking off our costumes, we are walking around as pseudo-selves, which no longer serves the organization going forward.

Albert Einstein said, "We can't solve problems by using the same kind of thinking we used when we created them," and "What we have called matter is energy."

Each of your team members is an energy being, and it's time for us to accept that in the corporate world. We need to leverage this knowledge when we are dealing with our teams and be able to use this information to move us forward in a way that has never been done before in strategic planning, from an energetic level with in-the-moment presence.

∼

I was born Jivi Saran in Mission, British Columbia (BC), Canada, and I lived there for a couple of years with my parents and my entire extended family. I moved with my family to Surrey, BC, in 1972 and stayed there until the age of seven, when my sister and I were sent to attend Shivalik Public School in Punjab, India, for seven years. I returned to Canada to complete Grade 12 and then spent a year in India after my arranged marriage.

I moved back to Canada permanently with my husband in 1991 and we settled in Surrey. I have two of the most wonderful children in the world, my daughter Neena and my son Raj, now young adults. In 2010, I moved to Nanaimo, where I reside with my children today.

For thirty years, I have been in healthcare, performing organizational development work through strategic leadership, team development, and change management roles. My educational background includes completing a PhD in Spirituality and an MBA specializing in Leadership Studies. I have built my credibility through authenticity, humbleness, and creative problem-solving skills. I have been acclaimed as a phenomenal keynote speaker and an engaging trainer and coach who quickly meets and exceeds the expectations of any work environment. Seeing people change and grow in their professional and personal lives gives me the gratification that fuels my motivation for high personal performance. I am known to connect with people easily, to understand their values and motivators quickly, and to develop programs and training to ensure they thrive in their work environment. The industry has said that, as an Organizational Development Consultant, I build a strong foundational relationship that is based on trust and respect, all the while creating a safe environment for people to be authentic.

Join me as I tell you about my life. I hope that my journey to authenticity will help you to find your own.

Chapter 1 Not Wanting to Turn On the Lights

As I sit here looking out at the Pacific Ocean in my beautiful home, I am reminded of last year at exactly this time. I had left a full-time corporate job and found myself sitting with a life coach, feeling lost, confused, resentful, sad, and with no clear direction for my life. I did, however, know that the way I had lived and worked had created an emptiness in my heart that I could not explain.

Is this all there is to life? What do I have to account for the last forty-four years of my life? Where do I go from here if I truly want to live my soul's purpose?

My career had come to a screeching halt and I knew that my path would be different going forward. I just didn't know how, what, where, or even why. I had worked in healthcare for thirty years. How could I feel disconnected from the only work I had known since I was sixteen years old? I was at the peak of my career, with great colleagues and fulfilling work, and yet there I was, sitting with a life coach, feeling as though I knew nothing about the future direction of my life.

A Journey down Memory Lane

Let's take a journey down memory lane.

When I think back, these exact feelings were what I experienced at the age of seven, when my parents sent me to attend a boarding school in Punjab, India. I remember feeling lost, confused, resentful, sad, and fearful the very first day of boarding school. I did not understand what was happening.

Imagine for a moment a boarding school dormitory with a hundred single beds, each an arm's length apart, as though in a long hallway. Each bed was the exact same size and shape and was made up with exactly the same bedcover in the exact same color. There I sat at the edge of a single bed in the middle of this empty dorm—a seven-year-old girl with my four-year-old sister, Neeta.

Many thoughts went through my head. "Are they coming back to get us? Are we staying here forever now? What do we do now? Where are all the other kids?"

Feeling lost, abandoned, nervous, and scared, we sat quietly without saying a word to each other, just staring at the metal trunks numbered S550 and P551 containing all our belongings. Those numbers became our identity for the next eight years.

It is interesting thinking back now. What could we have said to each other? There was nothing to say.

The unpleasant details I remember are the mealtimes at the canteen, the teachers whom we loved to hate and, above all, "Why?", my eternal question. "Why would my parents do this to us?"

Very often when I recited this story to others later, it ended up being a story of trauma, devastation, betrayal, sadness, disappointment, confusion, loneliness, loss, and loss of control; but amid everything else was the confusion of not understanding why. I would recite my story, saying things like, "the boarding school was horrible; the food was disgusting; we had no free time; we were woken up every morning at 4:30 a.m.; we missed our parents; we had to copy letters to our parents off a blackboard; every letter was audited before it was mailed out."

I held some deep resentment toward my parents for sending us there, resentment that showed up as passive-aggressive behavior on my part later in life. "It's not like I feel a part of this family anyway," I would often say.

Then one day as I recited my story probably for at least the hundredth time, my friend asked a question that would change my life forever. She said, "Jivi, what will it take for you to change your story?"

"Huh, what will it take to change my story? I love my story. That is who I am and why would I change 'the truth'? That's what actually happened!"

After an emotional outburst, I sighed deeply and followed that with a realization: I had become my story and had eagerly adorned a victim costume!

This question ate at me for a few weeks, leaving an unsettled feeling in the pit of my stomach. I started to look into this story through a different lens. What am I missing? Why am I so comfortable wearing this costume? What purpose is this victim story serving for me, and why am I unwilling to let this story go?

But the epiphany came when I asked myself, "What did I gain from that experience that makes me who I am today?" Maybe that was when I remembered more of the events.

Hard-Working Parents

Working hard and having little regard for self-care is learned, mimicked behavior that we pick up from our surroundings and our upbringing. My parents were very hard workers, as they had emigrated from India to Canada for a better life. I remember most of my life they worked twelve- to fifteen-hour days, if not longer. I rarely heard them complain about anything, and to be very honest I can't even really recall a time when they were sick. Taking time from work meant there would be no income, so they rarely missed work, especially because they owned and worked side businesses for extra money. Their hard-work value system meant they could provide financial support to all of us—me and my sister and brother. In those times, there simply was no concept that you could make a living doing what you love to do. Work was work, and its main purpose was to provide finances for the daily running and functioning of the home.

People Pleaser

The day I was leaving Canada at the age of seven to go to India, I remember sitting at the edge of the bed with my father and him saying to me, "Do you know why we are sending you to India? Because we want you to be somebody and we want to be proud of you."

I spent the rest of my life trying to make him proud without realizing the toll it was taking on me.

Spending Time with My Grandparents in India

When I was growing up in India, during our boarding school holidays I spent a lot of time with my maternal grandparents in their home in the village. As I think back, I was such a people pleaser. I would wake up early in the morning to help milk the cows and do other errands around the house. Not because I was being asked to, but more because I wanted to please my aunt, who lived there as part of my extended family.

Looking back now, I see that it was quite funny, really. She would say to me, "Wow, Jivi, you make the best lentils," or "You hang the clothes out for drying the best." And this small amount of praise would make me so feel so proud that I would do even more. I would wake up first thing in the morning, eager to please. After helping with milking the cows, I would sweep the floors and then sit down with my grandmother to make breakfast.

Back in those days, we used to wash the dishes with ashes from the stove; it was called "dry washing." So, we would take the ashes from inside the stove and rub them on the pots and pans instead of using soap, and then rinse everything with water. I was always super excited to do this "because I wash the dishes the best."

It was not the easiest thing to do, to live without my parents in someone else's home, because I had a constant desire to prove myself. I missed them when I was sick and yearned for them deeply, at least for the first few years, and then I began to lose interest in them. It was no walk in the park for them either, I am sure. After many years of feeling rejected, betrayed, and angry, I finally realized that they did what they thought was best for us at that particular time.

This people-pleasing part of me showed up years later at work, in doing extra work, longer hours, and wanting to be the best and the most perfect at each project. We are so good at mimicking our past in our future without even realizing that is what we are doing.

Do you see how it is inevitable that we carry our story into the work environment, whether we know it or not? Each story is a patch on our costume that we wear for society, and before we know it, we are wearing a full costume of all the stories that we think define who we are as people.

This same Jivi who was so eager to please others also did the same thing in her home environment. Always going out of her way to do things for others without even considering the cost to herself, all so that people would think, "Jivi is a good person."

It was as though I had good-person syndrome.

It wasn't until a few years ago that I finally started to learn how to say no to people, and still it's the most awkward thing for me to say.

Monkey Steals Grandfather's Bell

I would spend my afternoons in the holidays talking at length with my grandfather about life and his life lessons. For most of my childhood, I grew up with his stories about the significance or insignificance of life. He was an elegant storyteller; he is most likely the person from whom I get my gift in storytelling. Many of the stories I tell are about him.

My grandmother, on the other hand, was a quiet woman, very strong in essence and an extremely hard worker. She rarely rested when everyone else was sleeping in the middle of the day. They had a beautiful relationship, each of them doing their specific part to keep the wheels of the home moving efficiently.

When I was younger I did not really understand the morals of most of Grandfather's stories, but as I grew older and started to experience my life, I was constantly reminded of his stories until finally they made sense. Unfortunately, he was not around to see the lightbulb go off in my head.

One such story came many years later, after my grandmother had passed away. I went back to visit my grandfather. I asked him how he was and, as he usually did, he answered, "I am like a man in a story.

"Once there was an old man," he said, "and his wife died. His wife was a great caretaker of this old man, to the point at which the old man had almost forgotten how to take care of himself. His wife would make wonderful meals in special ways

Chapter 1

and she would serve them to him when he arrived home from doing farm work. Upon his wife's death, the old man was lost without her and was grieving quietly in his heart.

"Now the story changed," Grandfather said. "First the grandkids would bring him his food to wherever he was sitting in the home. Now, when you're old," he said, "You have many needs. The family began to get sick of the old man. So, one day, the old man was approached by his son, who said, 'Father, you should probably come to the kitchen to eat. Everyone is busy and they can't be running around trying to find you all the time.'

"So, the old man started coming to the kitchen to eat.

"Next, the old man had a bit of a cough, and when he would come to the kitchen, his daughters-in-law would get upset that he was coughing and spreading germs. So once again, his son made another request of him. It wasn't really a request—more like an order. They had set up a bed for him under a banyan tree far away from the house, and they gave him a bell to ring when he needed something.

"Every time the old man rang the bell, a grandchild would reluctantly present himself to help his grandfather, but not without making sure the old man knew how busy everyone was and that he was being a disturbance to their life.

"One day, the old man woke up from a nap and could not find his bell anywhere. When he looked up into the banyan tree, he saw a monkey with his bell. The grandfather had a look of dismay on his face."

My grandfather concluded the answer to my question "How are you?" with "Today I am like the old man whose bell was taken by the monkey."

I came to realize in my later years that Grandfather was talking about how our children treat us when we get old and are no longer of any value to them. All of a sudden, the simplest of things that become a necessity for someone older become an inconvenience for the younger generation.

Many of my grandfather's stories like this put my life into perspective, and they continued to do so well after his passing away. These stories are sewn into my costume and have become lessons for me as I journey through my life.

He told a special story that our body is simply a vehicle traveling on this road called life and that we will encounter rainbows, sunshine, flowers, cemeteries, hospitals, births, and deaths as we journey, and they are all a part of this journey. I am reminded of this each time I deal with happiness or sorrow. I am reminded that I am simply a vehicle passing through this earth, gaining experience.

More Selfless Giving

I can pinpoint very specific flashbacks in my life when I was doing something from this good-person mentality, yet not even wanting to do that something. I yearned to be different from how I was—I would look at others around me who could easily say no to things and I would think to myself, "Wow, how I wish I could do that," or "I wish I had the guts to say that," or "If only I could get away with doing that."

This internal battle ate away at me inside. I wanted to be like others and yet in the same breath I would behave contrarily to what I desired. "Give, give, give" had become my motto and I thought to myself, "They will get it one day and say I am a good person. It's only a matter of time. I live through my heart and that should be enough, no?"

What I did not realize was that people can give so much that, one day, they sit there completely empty and unhappy, not even knowing why. That was happening to me. Deep down inside I knew exactly how I wanted my life to be. I knew exactly what I wanted to change. I knew exactly what my desired state would be, and yet I fooled myself into believing my reality right then was exactly the way it should be.

Today, I say to people, "If you are fooling yourself that the current state of your affairs is okay, at the very least, do it with conscious awareness. Don't be untruthful to yourself."

A Different Story Today

Today I share this story of my years in India differently. I tell of having strong friendships, doing homework together into the wee hours of the night, sitting around a fire together, learning the power of prayer and meditation. I describe teachers who were willing to go the extra mile. I speak about being in leadership roles; I describe being in the National Cadets and on the debate and dance teams; I describe participating in stage plays; I talk about having computers and solar panels in the mid-1980s; I describe eating the best food possible for a thousand kids!

Today, I share a new story, one that does not require a costume or validation by others. It's a new story that has taught me about teamwork, leadership, conflict resolution, commitment and, above all, love for complete strangers. One that has taught me we don't need our stories to adorn our costumes, nor do we need to validate each other's costumes. One that has taught me I am who I am. And nothing more and nothing less shall I be.

With the new story, a new Jivi emerged—a Jivi who tells the story of survival, courage, strength, persistence, and resilience.

My story started to shift, but not without its challenges, because if I was not the person in the story, then who was I?

As the costume I had worn for decades started to slowly come off, I was left feeling vulnerable, raw, and exposed. Confused, I began a journey of recognizing the costume. It took a leap of faith to be vulnerable without this costume, and finally to take off the costume and to be who I am in true and pure form.

This was no easy journey, because that costume fitted me so well—the stitching was perfect, the colors were perfect—and so many people had validated my costume for me. "Wow, Jivi, how did you survive being away from your parents? That must have been tough!" That's when I realized I had been wearing a victim costume all my life, a costume that validated my story and had me remember only my worst perception.

Reflection Thirty-Seven Years Later

How could it be that in 2015, thirty-seven years after starting at boarding school in India, here I was in the exact place in my heart? What was the connection? I was determined to find out, and I started "turning on the lights."

Having to go back and look at each segment of your life is not an easy deed to accomplish; you have to be willing to look at your truth, to desire to see the full picture and, above all, to be courageous enough to look at things that you have put in the darkness for a long time. Sometimes, these very dark rooms have pain associated with them, and therefore we feel it's best to leave them in the dark and not turn on the lights. I am here to tell you, as much as it's the most difficult thing one can do, turning on the lights is also the most rewarding. The reward comes in the form of being truly aligned with who you are and who you are meant to be.

Often I heard or read advice such as "Do the inner journey," "Just go inside yourself," or "The answer is within you," and I found myself scratching my head. I then wished there were a canoe I could get into and paddle through my brain, turning the lights on in all the rooms I had left in darkness. I used to think that would be an easy task. However, turning on the lights requires patience, courage, and being prepared to embrace your emotions.

The beauty in turning the lights on does not reside in remembering what you already know; it resides in looking at each story from a different angle. Each time, it gets easier than the last time, but not without some level of emotion. Turning on the lights in our life requires us to pay attention to how each situation is intertwined with how we show up to work and our life in general.

For me, turning these lights on meant that I could now reach out for healing and support so that I would never allow the room to be dark again. It meant searching for the healers who became part of my healing support network. The real work began with me, and I was thirsty enough at this point to desire something different, a truer me, a more authentic me, a self who is in control of her own actions.

How to Turn On the Lights

When you are ready, willing, and open, the healer, the mentor, or the guide will present themself. You simply have to surrender to the Universe, and believe me when I say this, it is easier than it sounds.

There are many ways to practice turning on the lights to all the dark places in our life. Start to become the observer of your own story and, just as with any story, start from the beginning of time, just the way I did, from describing myself sitting at the edge of the bed at boarding school at the age of seven and thinking forward into my life today. Each story carries a perception of pain that we hold onto, thinking it is necessary. The perception of pain that we have about facing our so-called demons is not real; it cannot be real, because each of those experiences has made us who we are. Just like dots on a graph that tell a story once plotted, your life path will tell a story once all the darkness is gone.

You could share your story with a friend with whom you feel safe and ask them to simply listen and ask you questions without giving you advice. You could write your story in a journal, or join a peer mentoring or a coaching group.

Exercise—Mind Mapping

One method I found very helpful and continue to use is maintaining a mind map journal. I have never really liked journaling by writing long paragraphs, so mind mapping works perfectly for my style of processing information.

Take an empty piece of paper and in the center write the topic of the story, just like some of us did in brainstorming in school when writing an essay. Think back to the stories you tell the most frequently and select one story to focus on. Now, write everything that comes to mind on this mind map journal about the story. Leave out absolutely nothing, even the parts you really don't want to admit to yourself.

Ask yourself some of these questions as you mind map this story.
- What elements am I missing here?
- What are some of the key things I remember vividly and some of the things I may be forgetting?
- What feelings come up for me as I think about this story?
- Who else was in the story that I may be forgetting?

- What else was going on in my life at the exact same time as this story?

When you start to process a story from all angles, not just from your current truth, you will come to see that there were many angles to that story and you had chosen to see only the ones that may have justified your truth and validated your part in the story. There were probably many other things going on at the exact same time that may have influenced the choices or decisions that you made.

Just as with my boarding school story that went from resentment and confusion to making me who I am today with courage and warrior skills for life, your story will show you exactly why it happened in the moment that it happened. It was perfectly, divinely guided to make you, you. When I look at my life today, I see it is based on being in Universal flow and the present moment, being accountable for my actions and for my financial freedom, and knowing the impact I have in the lives of other people. It is entirely different from the first story you read about me.

Today it's time to take the first challenge and to be willing and open to turning on the lights.

Exercise—Lights On

Name one person whom you can trust implicitly to share aspects of one of your stories. Ask if they would be willing to help you in a process of self-discovery, the intended outcome being you want to learn from your story and move on. Their role is to simply listen and ask the questions below. Give them this questionnaire ahead of time so they have time to read it over before you chat.

Advice for Listener

As a listener of the story, pay attention to gaps in the story that don't make sense and ask, "Can you tell me more about that? There seems to be something missing."

Do not offer advice or solutions.

Listener's Questions

1. From your perspective, what happened in the story? Simply start with "According to me, this is what happened."
2. Who else was involved in the story?
3. If they were asked to recite the same story, what do you think they would say?
4. What parts of this story are absolutely true, something you have heard or seen yourself?
5. What parts may be hearsay?
6. What elements may you be missing as a part of this story?
7. What is one thing about this story that makes your heart heavy, something that you wish you could make go away?
8. What is one thing that you just learned in retelling this story that you did not remember before? Does that memory impact the story? How?
9. What is one thing you wish you could go back in time and change about yourself in this story?
10. If this story had not happened, what are five things that you might have lost or not experienced or not learned?
11. Are there any actions you can take now that would help support forgiveness of yourself and others?
12. The next time you encounter something like this, what will you do differently?

Chapter 2 Shackled by Limiting Beliefs

Back to Canada

Without any warning in 1986 at the end of Grade 10, my parents arrived to take us back to Canada. I was devastated, because India was all I had known to be my home.

I felt empty. There were many life experiences that led to this place of emptiness, this place of living for others and acting as the social worker for everyone. I was always trying to please other people because of my fear of rejection. This fear of rejection had its roots in the stories I told myself about being sent to India in the first place, and now coming back to Canada in Grade 10. I was resentful. Somewhere along the way of pleasing everyone else, I had lost my own identity of who I was meant to be.

Petty News Stories in Canada

Soon after I arrived back in Canada, I remember walking into the new corner store my parents had built. Right in front of the store was a newspaper box and on the front page was an article about some challenge with the Pacific National Exhibition fairgrounds. To provide some context, I had arrived from India just two years after the Blue Star Operation, the attack on the Golden Temple, and the assassination of Indira Gandhi.

The newspapers in India had been filled with graphic articles about hundreds of people being killed every day for the last few months. There were curfews at night; no one came out of their locked rooms at night for fear of being killed. It was a political and religious civil war in which many innocent people lost their lives.

So, there I was, having just arrived in Canada, staring at a newspaper and thinking to myself how ridiculous and irrelevant this news was. I have to say, I even experienced a level of disgust and anger that people would even consider this to be worthy as front-page news, let alone worthy to be on an inside page of the paper.

"Why would my parents consider bringing me back to Canada?" I thought. "This country doesn't even know what 'real news' is."

I was off to a pretty good start with the blame game, wouldn't you say? This was just the beginning of my lack of tolerance and my judgment toward the Canadian system of living. When you're in a place of wanting to blame anything and everything for your own misery, you will find even the smallest thing to blame; it doesn't even have to make any common sense.

Next, the Canadian education system amplified my feelings of judgment. Then, I started school and was put into a lower grade than where I had been in India, with the school citing the fact that the education system is inferior in a "third world country." When I began school, though, teachers quickly realized that what they were teaching me in Grade 10, I had completed in Grade 6 in India. So I was moved up to the appropriate grade.

When I think back, going to school in Canada was rather surreal. I did not really fit in and I felt a difference in the level of maturity between myself and the other kids. They had not experienced the environment I had, and I felt ill-prepared to handle my new environment. I should have reflected my anger at my parents and talked to them about bringing me back to Canada after knowing India as my home for so many years. But no; it was easier to blame things I had no control over.

I had a couple of years in the Canadian education system and found a close group of friends who understood that I could not go to parties or just out with them after school, because of my cultural upbringing.

Grade 12 was when I started to really get noticed by people, because my parents had purchased a grocery store near the school. That was an opportunity for kids to come to the store to get free candy, gas, or pop. I was literally two different people: one happy, jolly person who attended school and another miserable, unhappy person who went home to my family. I put my family through a lot that year, lots of disconnection, detachment, and overall not acting like a part of the family. I guess that's the way most teenagers are sometimes, and my teenage years were coupled with hidden resentment, anger, and disappointment. Listen to the beat of your own heart. Yep, that's exactly what I was doing, all right. My heart was sad and angry and that's how I was behaving.

Living in Duality, Even at Work

I was carrying this heavy burden of blame into my work environment as well. My first job in Canada, at age sixteen, was working part time as the medical receptionist in a physiotherapy office.

Two very significant milestones from that workplace have impacted my life. One day, around nine in the evening, we were closing up the office for the night. My job at night was to make sure all the rooms were clean and prepared for the morning, as well as to mop all the floors. I finished mopping the floors and went to ask the physiotherapist where I should dump the dirty water from the bucket. He directed me to dump it in the toilet, and as I poured the water in, the toilet self-flushed due to the water pressure. This totally makes sense now, but then, I was shocked! As I stood there in disbelief, the physiotherapist called out for me and asked, "Jivi, what happened? Are you okay?"

My response stimulated the most epic milestone in my life. I said, "You are not going to believe this. The toilet just self-flushed!"

And he stood there for a moment with a puzzled look on his face and said, "Jivi, sometimes I think you are much more intelligent than your age and sometimes I am reminded of how naïve and stupid you can be."

This statement stuck with me all my life because it points out the duality created by living in two countries. Some things came easily and other simple things, I could not understand.

The other significant incident involved a young woman who also worked there during the day as a receptionist. She was my first friend in Canada, someone who really taught me slang English and some basic things about Canadian society and culture. I remember her being shocked that I came from a large joint family consisting of my grandparents, my mom's brothers, and their families—approximately ten people—all living together in one very large home. I was equally shocked that she and her husband lived by themselves. I couldn't comprehend how her household would even function with only two people.

Then came the day when she gave birth to a little baby boy and I asked her what she had decided to name him. She had named him D.J. Curious, I asked, "What does that stand for?"

She responded, "Dukham James."

I again was in disbelief. This was all so strange to me. I kept thinking, "What was she thinking? What does that name even mean?" In India each name has a meaning and we believe that you live out the meaning of your name, so everyone is very careful about what they name their child. "How could she be so mean to her child?" I thought.

Intolerance and Blame

I was filled with intolerance, a lack of understanding and, to top it off, so much blame. I blamed my parents for bringing me back to Canada; I blamed Canada itself for not knowing how hard life is; I blamed this young mom for naming her child what she wanted his name to be! Wow, was that ever a solid example of misplaced anger! Each of these scenarios increased my judgment of others without realizing that they had not been brought up in India and they had their own traditions, values, and culture here in Canada. Having lived in India, its culture was my only measurement of how society functions.

My frustration and blame were in full force that year, with each situation validating exactly how I wanted to feel—angry, frustrated, sad, and disappointed with the world. Sometimes, we truly don't even realize what we are doing or reacting to. I had no idea during those years of how obliviously I was living my life. How could I have done differently, given my age at the time?

When circumstances continue to change as the years go by and I am the only constant, it becomes very apparent what the issue actually is. It's me! Mirror, Mirror on the wall, who am I among these all?

Let's take a deeper look into why it is so difficult to look at ourselves and the role we are playing, rather than blaming all our circumstances. First of all, there was an absolute disconnection between me and my knowing that I was blaming others for all my problems. That knowing was not even in my conscious awareness. It was years later, when I processed my life, that I realized how foolish I truly had been in those days. When I looked back at my life, I realized it was a series of blamings and deflections from the truth. The truth was hard to handle, not just for myself, but also to share with the people whom it needed to be shared with.

If you don't have something nice to say, don't say it, all right? I did not have anything nice to say, so why say it? I was better off being quiet. What I didn't realize in that moment was that everything I was holding inside was like a mini volcano that could erupt any time, either through my being verbally angry or through showing up as ailments in my physical body. The withheld energy had to go somewhere, so it festered and boiled inside my body.

Running Away in Grade 12

My ignorance of the world is very apparent to me now as I reflect back on one particular story, when I decided I was going to run away from home. I had decided this with my best friend in Grade 12. I was done with everything and everyone. I had a great plan: I would move in with her, I would go to the same high school, and I would do all the same things I regularly did, just not from my home. Just for context, I will tell you my friend lived down the street from me with her mom. Very logical, right? Not so much!

I wrote a letter to my parents telling them I was leaving home. To be honest, I can't really remember what exactly I wrote in that letter. I left it with my sister with very specific instructions for her to give it to them after I left. My friend came to pick me up with my clothes and some other small things. Oh, and of course my Christmas presents because it was December and who was going to open them there? We left quietly from the back door.

We drove to her house and placed all my belongings in a bedroom in her basement suite and then decided it was a great idea to go the mall, which, I might add, was fifteen minutes from where we lived. The naivety and ignorance in this entire situation is really funny in one sense, and yet it was a devastating sense of betrayal to my parents.

As we sat at The Pantry restaurant eating dinner with our friends and planning out how I would enter school on Monday, a friend who worked across the hall in the mall came to us and said, "Jivi, your dad was just here in the mall looking for you."

In that moment, I realized how stupid all this had been. What was I thinking!

We quickly finished our food and headed back to my friend's house and, as we pulled up to the driveway, we saw my father and my uncle waiting there. My father did not say much. He simply asked me to get my things and get in his car. I didn't know fear until I was staring my father in the face in such a situation. I went downstairs and gathered my things, which I had not even unpacked yet, and without saying a word got into his car.

When we arrived at home, he asked me to go my room until the next day. As I passed through the family room to get to my bedroom, my extended family sat there and watched me without saying a word. That evening, I could hear everyone talking in the family room. They were saying that I had probably run away with some boy. Really, I thought to myself, if that were the case, would I have gone ten houses down and been at the mall fifteen minutes away from home! The next morning, I woke up and left for school without anyone saying a word to me about what had happened the day before.

To this day, I don't know what everyone assumed happened in the nine hours I was away, but the series of events that came next lead me to believe that they thought I was in love with someone and planning to run away with him.

University or Marriage

My parents' fear of losing control of their daughter was high enough that this incident in December 1987 soon led to conversations about my marriage. I had "gotten out of control" and I was faced with a choice: get married the next summer or go to university. Guess what! Getting married seemed like a walk in the park, at the time. I felt as though I had become a problem, and it was best for this problem to be someone else's issue.

Limiting Beliefs

We as human beings have trained ourselves to think within a certain boundary. We take up very little space in the world, whereas we are actually here to experience big things and take up a lot of space. We get bound by certain models that exist within us and certain systems that run our lives. Before we know it, we are unhappy with the status quo. Expanding ourselves past what we know to be our comfort zone requires courage, and when we get stuck in mundane thinking, we cannot even find that courage.

I would hear people talk about how to better your life, how

to be happy, and how to live the life of your dreams. I went to hundreds of conferences, heard unlimited speakers, and took many courses, yet my life seemed the same. Things changed for a few days because I would leave the conference with some drive, and then I would come home and before I knew it, life would go back to being exactly the same as before. I was aware that I wanted to change my life, and I was building up my knowledge, but where I fell short, ultimately, was that the changes I needed to face had consequences. Therefore, each time, within a matter of days, I once again settled into the very life that I despised. I needed to find something special.

Magical Pen

One day as I sat staring at the lines on my hand, I considered seeing a palmist. "A palmist would probably be able to tell me what I needed to know, give me the answers, right?" I reached out to one of my spiritual mentors and asked him, "Do you know a good palmist that I could see?"

He responded, "Yes, I knew one a few years back, but he died recently, probably because he could not predict his own death!"

I sat there for a few minutes, reading between the lines. I guess no one knows our personal destiny and it's all up to us to create it. So, I picked up a pen and traced my hand on a piece of paper and started to draw out my life line, my love line, my health line, and everything else that I wanted in my life. I was holding the magical pen I came destined with to create my reality.

What if I told you that you came fully equipped with your own pen of destiny? Would you believe me? This is a magical pen that helps you change anything in your life story with some minor adjustments.

Our Limiting Beliefs

We are the only ones who limit ourselves into believing we cannot do something. We shackle our own hands and feet. If you feel that you are limiting yourself with beliefs that shackle you, try this exercise to identify what those beliefs could be.

> **Exercise—Breaking Free**
>
> 1. What do you think is absolutely impossible for you to do?
> 2. What makes you think that it is impossible?
> 3. What keeps you from trying it?
> 4. What limiting belief do you need to drop?
> 5. Select a date to take one small actionable step toward it, dropping this limiting belief.

Chapter 3 Paralyzed by Life Choices

The Strategic Plan for Your Life

Have you ever considered your life to be like a strategic plan that you simply implement each day, with goals just happening organically? With each of my stories above, you can see how life goals were being met without me even knowing. If you were to truly look at your life, you would realize it is one big strategic plan, with a strategic vision, the values you bring to the world, your goals, objectives, and milestones, their execution and evaluation, with mitigation and contingency plans. And then, of course, a celebration of your accomplishments.

Later, of course, comes our celebration of life. What is it that people celebrate about us when we are gone? What is it that we want people to celebrate about us? If something goes wrong in our life, like an unanticipated curve ball at work, how do we respond or react to the situation?

Having a strategic vision is crucial to the success of any business. If you don't know where you are going, how will you know you have arrived? Similarly, in our personal lives, if we don't know what's important to us and what our purpose is, how will we know what to fulfill? How many of us spend the majority of our lives asking ourselves, what am I here to do? What is my purpose or calling? We are great at creating vision statements for our businesses, so why does it become so difficult to do it for our personal lives?

When you consider a business, you can probably identify very quickly what value it brings to the world. I can tell you that my business brings value to people by inspiring them to be their true authentic selves at work. I can tell you that my business helps create even-minded people in the workplace so they handle their day with grace and ease. I can easily tell you that the value my business brings is creating happier workplaces so people are better contributors to the world and they go home happier.

Now, if you were to ask me, "Jivi, what value do you personally bring to the world?" you might have to give me a few days to ponder it through, and even then my answer might be clunky. I may not be sure, I may stutter, and I may not even be able to come up with an answer as easily as I can for my business value.

Consider for a moment: if you are one big walking, talking strategic plan, would you be able to clearly communicate your vision and the value you bring to the world?

Let's talk goals, objectives, and milestones. Do you have those for your personal self? Some of us might be able to articulate our goals, but can we go to the depth of knowing our objectives and milestones? If I were to treat myself as a business with a strategic plan, do you think I would be more likely to be successful?

When we are in the execution and implementation phase of a business plan, we think through each and every possibility, gather the appropriate resources, make a plan, and take action. Do we do that also for our personal strategy? Do we have mitigation and contingency plans for own lives, or do we even need them?

Manifestation Gap

With all these thoughts, I was not sure if I was expecting a genie to come out of the bottle and grant me the life I wished for. Or did I think someone would knock on my front door and give it to me in a nice little package?

This is where I fell short most of the time—not creating a solid personal strategy. I am great at creating a vision for myself that feels true to my heart, but then I realize all the work that needs to be done, and I often fall short due to the challenges that I could encounter. Why was it that I could easily implement either my own or someone else's business strategy, but when it came to my personal journey, each thought of wishing my life to be different from my current reality had me constantly in a place of unhappiness?

This is when I realized I was in a manifestation gap. I was falling into the manifestation gap between what my reality was and what my desired state would be. A manifestation gap is the place that we sit in when our desired state of being is different from our current reality and yet we do nothing or little about moving toward the desired state. We come up with every justification to make our current state perfectly okay so that we don't have to make the changes necessary to be in our desired state. I have to be honest, it felt a lot easier complaining about my life than doing something to change it. If I was not complaining about it to other people, I was definitely doing it internally to myself, through feelings of failure, guilt, sadness, and sometimes even self-sabotage. We don't even realize this game we play with ourselves.

My Father and I Head to India

In the summer of 1988, my father and I headed to India to "check out" a family friend who, it was felt, would be a good fit for me in marriage. Within a few days of our arrival in India, it was arranged that the family would come to our house and bring the boy whom they intended for me to marry. As he and my dad passed a window, I was to see the young man and decide if I would agree to marry him.

I watched them walk by. I watched my father and this young man walk by from a distance.

No way was I marrying this man, I thought. No way!

When my dad came into the kitchen to ask me my opinion, I said "This is not going to happen. He seems a lot older than me and he's not what I am looking for in terms of looks."

Frankly speaking, I thought he had a big nose. How shallow, I know. Don't forget, in this part of the story I am just seventeen years of age. I don't even know myself at this point, let alone what I want in a spouse.

My father told our friends of my decision and they left that day.

Here is where the story gets really interesting. The next day, the boy's family decided that if I did not like the first son they had offered me, then they had a younger boy who might be a better fit. They would like to come back and introduce him to me.

So, here we go again, with the second round. I couldn't help but think that it was like buying a car. If you don't like this one, maybe you could try this one?

The younger brother and I saw each other briefly from a distance; no words were exchanged. Before I had even said anything, everyone who had arrived with him started to leave.

Chapter 3

After they left, my father told me that the second boy had refused to marry me, citing that I was overweight and did not have the same education level.

This refusal to marry caused some chaos within my extended family at home. My relatives felt that their pride had been impacted because I was "refused for marriage."

"Now the whole village will be talking about this situation," they said, "and no one else will want to marry you."

Sit with that a moment. It was that their pride was hurt, not my feelings were hurt, or not that I was devastated that someone could be so shallow. Nope. Their pride was hurt!

Had anyone considered me? Remember me? I'm the one who is actually supposed to get married. It's also important to note here that my mom and siblings were still in Canada; it was just my father with his extended family feeling hurt.

If you thought this story was fruitless to this point, wait till you hear what happened the very next day. The next morning, there was a knock at the door and I opened it. There in front of me was the entire family that had come to see me the day before, though the boy I was supposed to marry was not there. They asked the whereabouts of my dad. I told them he had gone to town and would be back later that evening.

Later that evening, my father informed me that the same boy who had refused to marry me not even twenty-four hours earlier was "now ready to marry me."

Wow, a shocking turn of events, I thought. So my response to my father was, "I will not marry him without talking to him first. I want to know what has changed in twenty-four hours. Have I now become skinny and well-educated all of a sudden?"

The very next day, we met again. This time I was able to talk to him directly, with my aunt as a chaperone. I asked him what had changed in the last twenty-four hours that he now wanted to marry me. His response was simple: "I was just worried that I would not be able to finish my education and you were wearing too much makeup."

Okay, then, a simple explanation, but as I came to learn after many years of marriage, it was hardly true.

Not even a week later, on the Sunday, we were married—two people who clearly were not meant to be together and yet were paralyzed by family decisions.

This set the platform for a twenty-year marriage, from 1990 to 2010. Neither of us wanted to marry the other, but I said nothing to my family and if he did say something to his, no one listened. Don't think I am telling this story as a helpless female for whom a marriage was arranged without her consent; that is not the case. If I had said no to my father, he would have made a different choice, no doubt, but I still would have had a choice whether or not to marry.

This story is about not even knowing that no was an option and feeling paralyzed, feeling that marriage was inevitable and the only way for me. I had married for the wrong reasons, because I did not want to go to university and the only other option was marriage.

You would be highly mistaken if you think the Jivi in this marriage story did not show up in her workplace many years later. She absolutely showed up, in the form of feeling helpless about speaking her truth in meetings, reluctantly bringing forth ideas to the table, and attempting to stay under the leadership's radar so as not to attract attention to herself. My awareness of being overweight quickly became the reason for a lack of self-worth, self-confidence, and self-esteem.

We simply take how we felt about our experiences and project those feelings forward in different ways, but they still come from feelings that belong in the past. This continues to happen until you deal appropriately with your feelings.

Ours was a simple marriage at home, as at the time the political climate was not very good and only seven people were allowed to be at a public marriage gathering at any given time. I remember a few things from that day, such as the mirror breaking in the console on the bed; that became a constant reminder for me throughout the hardships of our marriage. Some money went missing and people were trying to find it. And I remember my dad taking me downstairs toward the vehicle I was going to leave in. It was a walk filled with sadness. We went down a long hallway and neither of us said a word. Only my father and I were in India; my mother and my siblings were in Canada. Looking back today, there was so much to say and yet nothing to say.

My Husband and I Live in India

When my husband and I married in 1990, he was completing his master's degree in botany in India. I knew immigration to Canada was a long process, so I decided to live with him and his family in India for a year. I loved living in India, having grown up in that environment. So, initially this was a godsend of an opportunity, until I found out that my husband would actually not even be home from Monday to Friday each week.

It was a fascinating time when I think back. He was away from Monday to Friday every week at university and returned on the weekends to study. So, I would spend time with his family, mostly talking to his grandfather about the historical partition of the British Indian Empire into India and Pakistan.

My husband's family was drastically different from others. So, not only was he not even home during the week, but I felt like an uprooted tree, adjusting to a new family. I find the concept of marriage intriguing, especially an arranged marriage. I was brought up in my Sikh culture to believe that I was someone else's property and that my parents were simply taking care of me. Then I married someone and I had a new family, a new last name, and everything that I knew to be somewhat true about myself was no longer true.

A new home, a new identity, and low self-worth created a great combination indeed. I would spend my days reading, talking, helping around the house where I could, and getting to know my new family. Looking back, I wish I had stayed in Canada, gained some education, found a job, and made some money. However, each time in our life is divinely guided, so I know I was meant to be in India for that period.

I learned a lot about myself that year—my level of patience, my tolerance and intolerance toward life, and the value of time. When my parents used to call me to see how I was doing, I would say, "Great. I'm sitting here counting bricks."

It had become a joke between us, because there was nothing else for me to do. There are times in my life that I just don't understand what I was thinking. This was one of those times.

Returning to Canada with My Husband

Each and every step in my life—from working in a shampoo factory capping bottles on a labor line and learning about my capabilities to grow and learn fast, to owning a janitorial business and learning humbleness, to cleaning restaurants and learning to be respectful of every stakeholder in a company, janitors included—was divinely guided for me to become who I am today. When I do business consulting today, I always include the business office's cleaners in my first meeting with the team.

Chapter 3

The first summer that I came back to Canada with my husband, we had just purchased a home and needed to make some money to pay the mortgage. We decided we would go berry picking in the local farms and looked for a farm where people would not know us. This was because we didn't want my parents to know that we were in that desperate a state for money.

We started off the first day in a strawberry farm not far from home. As you may or may not know, strawberries are the hardest berries to pick, as they are close to the ground. All day long, we either had to bend over or sit on our feet to pick them in the heat of the summer. When we came home that night, our bodies were in pain, we were exhausted, and we probably had heat stroke.

The next day someone told us about blueberries and how they were easier to pick, because you can pick them standing up. We decided this might be a better option for us, as I was pregnant with my first child and could not sit on the ground to pick strawberries.

We found a remote farm in Pitt Meadows and the owner was very nice to us. He said, "If you do well and pick the berries very fast, I will give the whole farm just to you for this season and will not hire anyone else."

Now, if you have never picked berries as a profession, you wouldn't know that this was great news for berry pickers. In other farms, the people who pick berries full time get first preference to the biggest berries, and since you are paid by weight, this is the best option for making money. We were honored and were eager to please him and show him how hard we could work.

On the very first day, we worked hard and picked berries as though there was no tomorrow. Before we knew it, we had picked as many berries as five people would have done in one day! Being so appreciative of our work, the owner gave us the run of the entire berry farm. Each day we would come to work prepared with our ice-cream buckets and tons of food. As much as it had become a challenge and we wanted to do the owner proud, we also started to compete with ourselves about how much more we could do each day.

"Okay, this was not as bad as our first day at the strawberry farm," I thought to myself. "I could handle this for the entire summer."

We were making great money, having a great time and, above all, we were working hard. After about two weeks, though, the excitement started to wear off. I was getting more and more tired, and often my husband would say, "Why don't you go sit under the shade of the tree and I will work for a few hours and we will just go home a bit later."

Sometimes as I sat there under the tree, I would think to myself, "This is not what I had imagined my life to be." I had to question what I was doing. "There has to be a better way to make money."

I had been very fortunate that my upbringing was one of financial abundance and I had not really been exposed to the hardships of suffering from a lack of money. As a matter of fact, I had not worked a day in my life before I got married, so this was all very new to me. I remember staring at the dirt, thinking, "If only my parents could see me now, dirty, hungry, tired, and pregnant."

Learning from the Farm Owner

One day, I was absolutely exhausted. I was almost four months pregnant with my daughter and I had been on my feet all day on a hot summer's day. As I sat there resting under the shade of a tree, I started to cry uncontrollably. The farm owner came and sat down beside me and asked, "What's wrong? Are you okay?"

As I sat there whimpering, I said to him, "If only my parents knew that I was picking berries today, they would be so mad at us, especially because I am pregnant. I am tired and I just want to go home."

He said something to me that day that I will never forget. He said, "My child, there is no shame in doing any kind of work, as long as you are the best at whatever you are doing. If you are a janitor, sweep that floor like it's the last time you will do it. If you are a magician, do the magic trick as though the whole world has their eyes on you. And if you are picking berries, do it as though it will give nourishment to some person in the world. It's not about picking berries; it's about nourishing the soul."

I have to say, I have given each job that I have taken since that conversation all I had to give; I gave it my soul. I will never forget that summer, as it was more than a job. We not only made $2,500 that summer, but we learned lessons that would serve us for a lifetime.

In the fall of the same year, we decided to open a janitorial business to serve restaurants and small businesses. We already had full-time jobs during the day as well. I was working in a medical practice as a medical office assistant and my husband was working in a pharmaceutical company as a chemist. Then we would market our janitorial business, going from business to business handing out business cards and flyers, and then during the evenings and well into the night, we would clean the establishments.

Life is about working hard to get ahead, right? That's what we thought at the time, that the longer and harder we worked, the better off we would be financially. I did not know how much the janitorial business would actually teach us about business models, marketing competitively, and customer service. It was a long stretch of work for a few years, and we definitely made some long-term clients.

Even though you may be wondering what this has to do with healthcare, hold on, because it has everything to do with my future career. The janitorial business taught me many things, among which is that you can't please everyone all the time, you can only be the best you can be on any given day, and to top it off, people use public washrooms in a very disgusting way, which they probably would never do at home! Other than learning about the lack of clean usage of public washrooms, you can clearly see how each skill can easily be transferred to any work environment.

Another major lesson during this time was about how operations are run and how they flow. I learned a lot about running a business from cleaning offices, such as methods for handling difficult clients, best customer service techniques, creative solutions to marketing and, above all, ways to handle a thankless job. Our janitorial business was harder even than berry picking, as in the farm you simply pick berries and don't have to manage various personalities and worry about losing the business. We would spend the entire night cleaning and then, first thing in the morning, we would get a call, "Did you happen to dust under the phone on my desk? It is dusty there."

I would often scratch my head in absolute wonder as to what people would notice when other things were clean. No one called us to say, "What a great cleaning job you did last night!"

We often don't realize how things from our past have the ability to shape who we are now in a positive way. When I started to work in an office, I would often leave thank-you notes on my desk for the cleaners and other little funny notes to make them laugh. I know how thankless a job they have and I made a point of making sure they knew their work was appreciated. As I had done janitorial services myself, I was better able to appreciate the work others did in the workplace.

Different Lessons

I learned in the shampoo factory about working hard and being the best that I could be, whether I was capping the shampoo bottles, putting the bottles into boxes, or making labels for the bottles. It was all about whether I could be the best at what I was doing on any given day.

Every one of these work environments was like a petri dish of learning lessons for everything that was to come on my journey. At the time that you are in it, of course, you have no clue that each situation is meant to happen in that exact moment in time, unless you are very in tune with yourself and, believe me, I was not. It would be years later that I could actually put all the pieces together and see how each circumstance is divinely guided.

In my personal life, every situation I've endured has made me stronger for the next challenge in my life. Each challenge became bigger, more difficult, more time-consuming, and sometimes the challenge even gave the perception of there being no solution. I believe that we don't see all the pieces as related because we are so busy and completely consumed by each situation individually and we literally ignore all the signs that are flashing in front of us. We get so caught up in creating a "happy life," we forget that all the unhappy times are when we grew the most, where we learned the most, and where we reflected the most about how to do things differently.

The learning I gained from the shampoo factory, the berry patch, the janitorial service—this was the Jivi who was showing up to work when I started to work in professional jobs. I remember doing my first keynote speaking engagement and sharing the story about being a janitor thirty years earlier in a medical practice. Everyone in the audience was shocked. "A janitor. Wow, I would have never thought," said one audience member at lunch.

I do my job best today *because* I was a janitor in a medical practice; otherwise, I would simply be speaking from books. Today, I speak from firsthand experience. Often, I would ask leaders, "Do you know the name of your janitor?" And upon getting confused and surprised looks, my response was, "If you don't know who makes your office presentable each day for your clients, you don't know your business."

Leading an organization and its people is about understanding that your leadership and business legacy is based upon acknowledgement that each person that touches your business has the ability to create impact toward your vision. If you nurture the individual, the individual nurtures your business; it's really that simple. Even though management and leadership are two sides of the same coin and each must have some role to move your business forward, it's time that we took a different angle and inspired people to be the best they can be on each given day. If each person in your organization is doing meaningful and purposeful work, they will do it with passion, and that passion is what becomes the driving force of implementing your strategic vision. Ask yourself these simple questions: Do you feel as though you are a valued contributor to your organization's vision? Are you being heard?

Exercise—Problem Paralysis

Close your eyes and think about one situation or problem or challenge in which you are feeling restrained. Then pick up any object from your surroundings; it can be literally anything—a candle, a picture, a bottle, a remote, any physical object.

Write down the top five characteristics of the object you have picked up. Consider the shape, size, color, and its use. Take each of these five characteristics and use it to come up with one creative solution for the situation in which you feel restrained. Before you know it, you will five different creative solutions to your problem paralysis.

An Example of Feeling Stuck in My Career and Using a Candle

I am feeling stuck in my career and I don't know if I should find another job. The object I pick up is a candle.

1. A candle is handy when the power goes out; it is a light source in darkness. What other career choices may be in the dark that I am not seeing?
2. A candle smells nice and can be used for aromatherapy. What kind of smell does this remind me of, nice or not nice?
3. Candles come in various colors. Are there other opportunities within the same organization that I could consider?
4. Candles are made from wax and wicks. Is it the job itself or the functions and tasks with the job that are holding me back?
5. There are many types of candles—organic and chemical. Do I believe in the core values of the organization? Do I want to leave because I don't like the job, or do I dislike the organization and what it stands for?

Chapter 4 Deep Yearning to Be Different but Not Knowing How

Many of us have this innate desire to be different in some way, shape, or form, whether by being healthier, wealthier, or even in a different relationship. This deep yearning inside us sits there eating away at us without our even knowing it. We set goals for ourselves and then if those goals are not met, we feel guilty and resent ourselves for not meeting them. How many times have you said to yourself at the beginning of the year, "I am going to get healthier, I am going to eat better, go the gym more, and really make myself a priority"? It works for the month of January and maybe even for February; then March comes around and we find ourselves in the same place again, not making time for ourselves. We get stuck in this vicious circle of setting ourselves up for failure each time that happens.

I would look at other couples and think to myself, "I wish my relationship with my husband were like that." I would look at healthy people and think, "I wish I could lose weight and look like that." I would look at successful people at work and think, "I wish I had my own successful business."

Managing with No Standard Operating Procedures or Guidelines to Follow

Soon after I moved back to Canada in 1991 with my husband, I started to work as a receptionist in a janitorial business that was setting up a new office in Canada. My job was to set up the business from scratch—doing the recruitment and training of staff and the scheduling of client work and setting up the office. I was doing a lot of what I call "white space work," which means there were no standard operating procedures or guidelines to follow; I was developing the operational logistics as we went along.

It was a great job, and I had worked there for about one year when one day the owner decided that the business was not as profitable as he had hoped, and he decided to shut down the office and move back to the States.

Right across the street was a medical management company's head office. Often, I would look out the window and wonder what they did in that office. One day, I decided to walk over at lunch and ask them what kind of company they were and what they did. I was very eager. The wonderful, bubbly receptionist informed me that they owned a series of medical practices across the Lower Mainland. As luck would have it—nothing is coincidence—I had just done some janitorial work for a medical practice in Vancouver, and while I was cleaning the office I had been fascinated, wondering what the medical office assistant was doing. I recall thinking, "I wonder what it takes to work at a medical office?" And here I was now, facing no job, and this bubbly young woman was more than willing to answer my questions. So, the conversation continued and I asked how one could qualify to work in a medical office, and she referred me to a very short Medical Office Assistant course that I could take in the evenings for six months.

I don't believe that all these incidents were unrelated: the location of the janitorial service office right across the street, the shutting down of the janitorial business, having just done some janitorial work in a doctor's office, and then of course meeting this lovely woman who was willing to share any information I needed. I asked her if I could come back and apply for a job once I had completed the course, and she was happy to accommodate my request.

If only I had known in that moment, standing there in front of her, that thirty years later I would reach the peak of my career in healthcare, having built credibility for myself. And that credibility would be based on the ladder that I worked so hard on climbing. To this day, I tell stories about my janitorial days in medical practices, as well as having experienced various other medical-practice roles, from being the janitor, receptionist, medical office assistant, manager, and director to the efficiency trainer for the medical office staff. This is the main reason for my success in my career.

A cousin of mine who worked in healthcare had been talking to me about a career in healthcare as well, and she was more than happy to help me find a role in the hospital. As destiny would have it, I failed the typing test for the hospital three times! If I had passed the typing exam, I would have started a career as an emergency entrance clerk and my life would have turned out completely differently. Failing the test was frustrating, and at the time I could not see how this was actually helping me set milestones for my future career in healthcare leadership.

Then I thought to apply to the nursing program and there just happened to be a two-year wait to get into the program. So I thought for the time I would take a job as a medical practice manager. I loved my role so much that when I finally got accepted into the nursing program, I declined my seat. Again, if that application had not had a two-year wait and I had gotten in right away, I would not have taken the job as a medical practice manager and my life today would be completely different.

At very pivotal points in my life where I was getting angry or upset that I was not getting what I wanted, it was actually meant to be in that exact way.

Feeling Emptiness Inside My Heart

Within this perceived perfect world that others thought I was living, I sat day after day feeling emptiness inside my heart and paralyzed by comparing what others thought was my life with what I was actually living. I would constantly question myself, "Am I missing something?" and "If everyone thinks my life is so perfect, then why don't I feel content and happy? Why don't I want to go home after a long day's work? Why do I feel disconnected from my husband and children?" Why, why, why? My life had become a series of questions. No matter how many psychic readings, tarot card readings, and spiritual channeling sessions I had with people, no one had the answers that could satisfy my questions. I felt like I was standing in quicksand, slowly drowning in my own paralysis. I knew that something had to change, but I did not know what, who, where, or how.

Emotionally Paralyzed

When we get emotionally paralyzed by what others perceive our lives to be, we start to believe that the life we are living is exactly what they want it to be. This same paralyzed person shows up to work each day carrying this level of misery to their performance at work. The same paralysis I was feeling at home showed up in my work environment as a paralysis in clear decision-making. It showed up especially in the mid-1990s as me not speaking my truth; it showed up as me always second-guessing myself and, above all, it showed up as my lack of self-confidence.

In my home life and at work I was in exactly the same place, and I could not identify that for myself in either situation. I had grown out of my personal and professional relationships and it was time to move on. I kept asking myself, which was true? The feeling that I had inside myself or what others were telling me? So, I stayed in both situations, thinking there was no other alternative or solution.

Why is it that we become so helpless and unwilling to look at why we feel stuck in a situation?

At home I would come up with excuses such as "The time is just not right. I cannot leave my marriage because my kids are little and there would be a massive impact on them. Because I do not know how to manage money, where would I go and how would I manage? I would not be able to live alone. What would my family think of me?"

Yes, any and every excuse became my very best friend. When my mom first found out about my divorce, she asked me, "Why now, after all these years of being together?"

I had one simply answer: "Because all these years I did not realize I was living out what everyone else wanted me to, and I didn't realize I was being eaten from the inside. Each day I was selling pieces of my soul."

At work it was the same situation, just a different context. The excuses were slightly different, but they came from the same fear. "Who will take my job? How can I leave the friendships I have made here? What if I am not smart enough for a new role? Who would want to hire me? What if I don't get along with my leader, my manager? I still love what I do. Leaving here would betray the person who gave me this 'golden opportunity,'" etc.

Many excuses. I am probably forgetting some, because believe me when I say it: I had a library of excuses to make my misery absolutely A-OK.

However, in neither situation did I realize the disadvantages of staying and the impact and the cost to myself. All I could see was the beautiful justification I gave myself for not having to change anything.

On a more personal level, my health was the worst it had been in years. I was overweight with diabetes and high blood pressure, and yet had "no time to go see a doctor." I had no time to exercise, no time to look after my nutrition, no time for self-care—so I told myself. This paralysis made me a prisoner in my own body, physically, mentally, and spiritually, with no release date in the future from this prison.

There is a milestone moment for some of us in of our lives that opens our eyes to how we are behaving. We suddenly realize our behavior is not aligned with what comes out of our mouth. My milestone moment hit me like a ton of bricks; it was the moment when I realized that I was in a miserable work environment out of obligation; I was in my relationship out of obligation; I attended parties, weddings, etc., out of obligation. My life had become one BIG obligation.

I Am So Busy

In the mid-1990s, "I am so busy, I can't even think straight" had become a fashion statement for me. I loved to say it when asked "How are you doing?" This would give the indication that, like the rest of the world, I was doing what I was supposed to do and meant to do, at full speed and at the cost of myself.

Yet secretly, inside, I desired something else, a day in which there were frequent breaks, a day in which I had an opportunity to read, go for a walk, do some personal development, write a book, and play with the kids. I would often think or say that I wanted to do some meditation, and yet when it came to making time for it, it simply didn't happen. This was another manifestation gap. My desired state was to meditate, and yet my reality was I made the excuse that I simply didn't have time.

Every time you give yourself the excuse of "I don't have time," give yourself a shake and ask yourself, "Do you not have time or is the thing you don't have time for not a priority for you?" A lack of time is the best excuse ever, because no one can counter you on it. What are they going to say? "You're lying; you do have time!"

Even though I was speaking this lingo of being busy, I would say things like, "I wish I had more time in a day," and "It has been crazy the last few days," as though that busy state was temporary and everything would be back to normal soon. I would rush in to work, rush to meetings that were booked back to back, rush to complete emails or other correspondence, and by then it was five o'clock and I was still sitting with my half-eaten sandwich from lunch on my desk.

"Diabetes and hypertension. I wonder where they could have come from? It must be hereditary," I would say to myself, even though it was five o'clock and I was staring at my sandwich from lunch, barely having had time to go to the washroom. That was another fashion statement I adorned proudly: "Time? What are you talking about? I haven't even had time to go to the washroom."

Being very clear that these are all fashion statements, there is absolutely nothing in your life that you cannot shift, should you really desire to change it. Now, if you don't want to change anything, that is perfectly okay. Just don't fool yourself into believing you want to change but don't have the time to do it.

Having read my description of my paralyzed state of mind, can you imagine how I would present myself in the workplace? Do you think I was paying attention to the details in meetings? Do you think I had fruitful relationships with my coworkers? Do you think I was able to bring to the table creative ideas about quality improvement? What I was able to do was to give a great performance of high productivity at a cost to my physical body.

High Blood Pressure and Diabetes

In 1998, I was diagnosed with high blood pressure and the doctors could not figure out why. Not very long after, I was diagnosed with diabetes. One day, I was in my doctor's office and I knew full well the conversation that was coming. "Jivi, you must lose weight," he said.

Yes, I kind of knew that already, but thanks just the same for pointing it out. We all know the spiel: eat better, exercise more, and reduce your stress. Now, think about this for a moment. If this were all that simple, would we all not be healthier? I had been overweight most of my life, and I had heard the message multiple times over the years, from my family, friends, strangers, and doctors. As a matter of fact, I had even heard it from my husband-to-be when he refused to marry me.

Each time I would encounter a conversation around weight, I would create this desired state of being skinnier. I would plan out exactly all the steps I "needed" to do. I would start doing them and then fall short again. So, if I knew that my diabetes and high blood pressure were directly related to my weight, why was it that I could not stick to "just losing some weight"? It seems logical that I should have been able to comply, right?

It's as though we start to live two lives—one that we actually are living and one that we should be living, according to everyone else.

My Epiphany Came Later

Many years later, post-divorce, I would have the greatest epiphany ever: what if being overweight were an indication of something deeper that was going on for me at a spiritual level? I realized I was holding onto extra weight to feel safe and secure, even from a biological perspective. My body was thinking, "Reserve as much fat as you can just in case she starves." As soon as I started to discover who I am and really live life the way I wanted to, the weight became a non-issue. After I left my marriage and moved to Nanaimo, I found myself walking every day. I found myself eating better and—wait for it—I found myself, for the first time in my life, losing weight and not even realizing it. People would comment about how I glowed. Years shed off me and I looked so much younger.

This realization that I was feeling and looking better and what the improvement was associated with did not come all of a sudden; it came with time. I was simply doing things that made me feel joyful, not because I had a particular outcome in mind. It was a couple of years later, when I would reflect back on that first year after my divorce, that the story all came together. Some of these learnings have even come together as I wrote this book. So, be kind and gentle with yourself as you go through your own journey. Remember that healing occurs in layers and sometimes even when you least expect it.

But I'm getting ahead of myself, because this realization took some time.

Sometimes we yearn for something but we want the wrong thing and don't realize it. We yearn for a change in our outer appearance, rather than really looking deep inside ourselves for what our soul calls out for.

Simultaneously with my epiphany, I knew in my heart that I was working too hard in my workplace. Putting in long hours and extensive amounts of work had become normal. I knew that my kids were missing me and I *should* be spending more time with them at home. I was fully aware that I had no work-life balance, and I would often desire the state of going home and being able to just play with the kids or peacefully have some time to myself.

The actual story was very different. I would come home tired, exhausted, and emotionally drained. I would enter my home and be extremely upset with the kids about leaving dishes everywhere or not doing their homework or not practicing their musical instruments, etc. No doubt the kids probably dreaded me coming home. I dreaded it myself.

One day as I was driving home, I thought, "What would happen if I missed the turnoff to my house and just continued driving down the highway? Where would I go?" I thought. "What if I could not take care of myself? What if I got into an accident?"

So many thoughts ran through my mind at the same time in complete duality. One line of thought was of running away, and at the very same time, I had the desperate feeling that I did not know how to be independent. As I continued driving down the road and intentionally missed the turnoff, I walked through every single scenario in my head of all the possible consequences, and then it hit me. "What would my kids do without me?" That thought alone triggered me to take the U-turn that quickly took me back to the very home that caused my discomfort and unhappiness.

If I had had today's maturity back then, I would have asked

myself, "What is it about my home that each day I do not want to go home?" And then I would have changed that situation. Yet, when you are in it and living it day in and day out, it's almost as though we really don't want to change the status quo for some reason.

Instead, I would stay at work longer hours, book meetings and conferences out of town, or book late dinner meetings—anything that would keep me away from my home.

We need to remember that I was not in an unsafe home. As a matter of fact, everything was exactly as it should be. The issue was with me. Instead of acknowledging that the issue was with me and with not knowing where the emptiness came from, it was easier to blame everyone and everything around me.

My Brother Asks Me a Question

One day, my brother came to visit and I asked him if he wanted to go for a walk with me. We ended up at the local elementary school on the swing set. He was much younger than I was, so his question took me by surprise. He said, "What is one thing that you regret in your life?"

My answer shocked me even more than his question. I said to him, "If it were up to me, I would live the life of a nun and find an ashram that I could dedicate the rest of my life to. I would not have gotten married."

Even as I said those words, I couldn't believe they were coming out of my mouth. Was this what I really desired? To live in an ashram somewhere? What I did not realize was that the ashram lifestyle was simply a metaphor for wanting to be at peace, to feel bliss, and to feel complete in some way.

Needless to say, we walked home quietly. I had exposed a side of me to myself that took me years to understand. Over the years of being in an unhappy marriage, instead of sharing with my parents what was really going in my marriage, I would often say to my mom and dad, "I wish I could just turn back time and be a kid again." I wanted to resign from adulthood. I had not found my voice yet, as to how to talk to them about it. I knew I entered my home feeling on edge and the smallest thing would set me off. My desired state of having a peaceful home was all an illusion for years.

I have had many coaching clients who express these same desires—to have more peace in their lives, more time with their kids, more time to be with their spouse, or to simply take time for themselves. Yet, each time we talk about how to get there, there are millions of excuses for how that desired state is next to impossible because of this, that, and the other thing. We are masters at making our current state exactly as it is and yet fooling ourselves into believing we desire another state.

I say this following sentence with love: If you truly desired a different state of being, you would do anything to make it happen.

Think back to some things that you thought were impossible. Maybe it was getting a certain client; maybe it was getting a certain project or a contract at work; or maybe it was even making time for a friend. I can almost guarantee that you made time for it, committed to it, and made it happen. If your will is strong enough, you will do what you set out to do.

So why is it that we have a yearning for a desired state and don't do it? Are we fooling ourselves into believing we are doing something about it when we actually have no intention to change anyway?

Having worked in change management for years, I have learned something very critical: we don't want to change, deep down inside, but we want others to believe that we like change because that's what we are supposed to say or think, right?

Chapter 4

I would go into organizations selling management on how fabulous the change was going to be, the benefits they would see, and I would even give them robust step-by-step change-management plans. Yet, in my own personal life, I had a secret: I could not accept change, even though I knew not changing was hurting me. Dual life, you say? You guessed it! From nine to five I was out there selling change, and then not wanting to leave work because I was unhappy to go home. What does that tell you about how talented we are about living two lives?

Once Life Works Well

I also want to share with you an example of how I showed up to work when my life was in balance and I was no longer doing things at my own cost. In my last workplace, understanding each team member was very important to me and vital to our success as an organization. The more I was in balance, the greater my output of work was, not just from a productivity perspective, but also from an emotional and spiritual perspective. I came to work joyfully and happily, and if someone else did not appear to be happy, I would ask, "What's going on for you? Want to talk about it?"

I could only ask this if my own state of mind was balanced. Otherwise, I would not be able to handle my own problems, so why take on someone else's? I felt relaxed, calm, and collected; therefore, it was much easier to be there for my team members.

Your state of mind is a direct reflection of how much you are willing to give to others. If you are "busy," how much will you be able to offer other team members—members, might I add, who actually implement your business's strategy and vision. In this state of balance it is easier to handle conflict, easier to spend time with things that matter, easier to handle my day with grace. My communication became much more effective. I was able to handle myself in tough situations with confidence. And the greatest benefit of all was that I was able to be myself in each situation, whether it was good, bad, or ugly. To maintain this balance for myself, I had to make some choices. I always took time away from my desk for lunch. I would take some calls as I went for a walk. I would always book thirty minutes between meetings; I had to be realistic with travel time between meetings. Monday morning was always left open for team calls in case someone needed something urgently. Friday was a no-meeting day; we did our team-mindfulness training on Friday afternoon.

There are some things that you have to stick to for your own self-care. This self-care then better aligns you to be a better leader for others. Your external environment simply reflects your internal environment. It's a hard pill to swallow when you know you, and only you, are responsible for your life as it is right now.

Strong Background in Prayer and Meditation

I grew up with a strong background in prayer and meditation. For at least four hours a day in India we would do some form of prayer or meditation. I recall the feelings of serenity, bliss, and mental clarity that I felt during those times. I also knew that I had a very deep connection to spirituality in the form of self-realization. Having experienced this state over a seven-year period—the years I was at boarding school—I knew I desired to be in that place once again where meditation and prayer were part of my day.

I had imagined in my head that prayer would take hours and hours out of my day, hours that I could be spending cleaning my home. Yes, you read that correctly. I thought cleaning my home was more important than cleaning my soul. As a matter of fact, cleaning my home had become more important than spending time with my family, my children, and even my friends. That's the one place I had any control over in my life, because I desired everything else to be different.

I knew in my heart that praying and meditating would give me exactly the answers I was searching for, and yet I still did not make time for it. What does that tell you about a person? Even experiencing firsthand the results of doing a certain action was not motivation enough for me to change and make that action a priority. Day in and day out, I showed up at work as this person with a conflicted personality.

This gap was not limited to my home environment. I also had a keen desire to do something for the world, to leave a legacy of sorts by contributing to making the world a better place. This enlightening moment came from a conversation with my coach. She asked me, "Jivi, what is a good day for you?"

It took me a few minutes to process the question because at first it seemed like I didn't know. Then it came to me: a good day for me was one in which I had time to read a book, do some personal development growth, spend time with my friends and family, and do something to better the world, like being involved in some worldly cause. What came from that question was a fascinating realization: "If this is the way I define a good day, let me be the first to say that I was not doing any of that in a day."

So, there I still was in a manifestation gap between how I wanted to be and who I really was. I would listen to the stories of other people who were living the life I desired, and yet I would say things like, "They wouldn't understand what I am going through. Their life is not as busy as mine. There is no way they would make it if they were in my life."

Why is that we think nothing applies to us because our situation is so unique? It is so unique that it is actually like everyone else's. Many of us desire peace, serenity, and a slower pace of life, and yet we do everything that is contrary to our desire.

There is a tipping point of that yearning sometimes. At some point it is forced by a medical diagnosis, a broken marriage, a tragedy that hits home, even a death of a loved one. Can we not attain our desired state without having to go through some level of devastation? There was also another very real issue for me—even though I knew that my current reality was making me unhappy, I did not know how to take the first step. And the repetitive questions would come: what if I was wrong? What if I leave the marriage and find out that I should have stayed? This story played out in my head again and again. I called it my "what if" story. You have to be in a place of "I will do what it takes to make my desired state happen at any cost." You have to be willing to lose things and be willing to gain things. You have to be willing to take the first step, and that's where you need to roar your greatest courage.

My Marriage Was Not Working

Looking back at a time in which my life was all about Excel spreadsheets, I had literally laid out my life in a ten-year plan. This was one place where I could have some level of control, or so I thought. There was a level of predictability in that plan, and the plus side was I was leaving nothing to chance. I thought I knew what I wanted and I had plotted it out exactly the way it would turn out. That's why we make plans, right? So we have some level of control and predictability.

But my life was turning out the complete opposite. Things I

had not predicted were happening in my life, throwing me off and causing me to be frustrated. The more I planned, the more the Universe unplanned.

I thought if I kept myself busy enough, I would not have to deal with the fact that my marriage was falling apart. My life was in an Excel sheet, from writing a book, hosting a television show, and maintaining my healthcare career path. To top it all off, I had written complete contingency plans, just in case one of these goals did not work out. No joke, I even had contingency plans for my contingency plans: for example, if the television show was not a success, I had a proposal ready for a radio show, and if that did not work, I had planned to purchase air time myself.

Looking back at those days, I realize they were twelve to fourteen hours long. I was at work for those hours during most of my career working multiple jobs. I was able to do that because my husband worked from home and was the main caretaker for our kids. I realize I kept myself so busy so that I did not have to accept what was not working in my life. I did not want to accept this because I knew once I accepted it, I would have to do something about it. And at this point of my life, I could not fathom the impossible—a divorce. A divorce would mean breaking with cultural and societal norms, having to disappoint my family, having to deal with the pain of the separation (which I interpreted as being lonely), and having to face my children. This felt destructive and unnecessary. "If I can just make it for one more year, the kids will be older and will be able to cope better, take care of themselves, and be less influenced by family."

My work was getting the best of me through long hours, my dedication to perfection, and my loyalty to my leader. Inside, unbeknown to me, there was a volcano ready to erupt. It did not take long before all the resentment and anger I felt at home started to manifest in the work environment through struggles with leadership, a short fuse for the simplest things, unhappiness with the way the program was running, and generally being miserable.

Here is the beauty of the situation. Everyone else could see a miserable person, but I could not see that I was the cause of my misery, because it was everyone else's fault, right? My work had started to become an obligation, just like my home. I had become a dysfunctional robot in both situations. I was making it work; this is what I was supposed to do, right? Keep my head down and deal with it, because "life is no bed of roses and you are strong if you just deal with it."

If I had only acknowledged that I had outgrown my marriage and my work, life would have been a tad simpler. Rather than doing that, I blamed others for my misery. I said my leader did not know how to lead effectively, my colleagues were not inputting at the same level of work I was, I did not have enough input into program development, there was more work to do in a day than I had time for. I wanted to be involved in everything at work and yet I complained about having no time. And then came the big one—I became passive-aggressive.

Then, of course, the same thing happened at home—my husband did not understand me, he wasn't giving me enough time, he made me feel inferior, he did not validate me enough, he was always too busy for me, he did not talk to me enough, he did not help me, etc. You get the drift. Do these sentences play out in your head like broken records? It's like a horrible song that has no tune, the words make no sense, and the singer has horrible vocals!

Every sixth of the month became a battle zone in our home. It was the day the credit card bill arrived. It always resulted in an evening of hurt feelings, unanswered questions, and loud voices that accomplished nothing. My feelings of resentment, guilt, and anger would start to build throughout the day, as I knew the bill would have arrived and my husband was going to ask me a series of questions ranging from "What is this item on the card?" to "Why did you spend this much?" to "What were you thinking?" I was prepared for battle each time and had my sword out before I even entered the house. His perception was that I was too lavish with my spending, and I was of the opinion that he was too frugal. Each month we repeated the same cycle of playing verbal tennis about how the other person was to blame.

It was easier to blame him; he was the horrible person here, right? It couldn't be me. Or could it? If only he knew what I actually snuck into the closet when he was not at home, calmly removing the tags, hanging up items, and acting as though I was surprised he didn't remember them. "This old thing? I bought it many months ago. Don't you remember?" I would buy things for the house and then tell him they cost a lot less than the actual price, so that he would not question me further. I would buy things with cash so there was no trace on the credit card, and these weren't even things I needed to hide!

What was I thinking? Why was all this perfectly okay? Relationships should be based on trust, right? As human beings we are masters at justifying our own actions, and I got an A-plus for my justifications. The answers to all these questions were trapped inside my reflection of myself. Here is where the light was not on. I was choosing to not want to get to know our financial situation, because I did not want to deal with the knowledge of having to be fiscally responsible. It was so much easier not knowing and just having a credit card that he paid, waiting for the battle on the sixth of the month, and moving on again.

No doubt the same Jivi showed up to work each day. So you are probably wondering how this manifested at work. Well, here it is. I did not want to handle budgets in my work environment and I stayed clear of any job descriptions in which I had to be responsible for budget projections. Yet, I was exactly the same as I was at home—I would rather complain about how we did not have enough resources to do the job. This became the battlefield at work.

In government, you are constantly up against budgets, re-allotted budgets, and reduced budgets. I chose to not build my knowledge around those budgets and how they worked, but I found it very easy to vent and complain about them. Both situations were exactly the same: a lack of wanting the knowledge because then I would have to be accountable for the choices in my life.

I thought this place of darkness was so much easier, as it allowed me to hide and continue to do exactly what I wanted to do rather than to deal with the fact that we had a mortgage to pay off and bills that needed to be paid. On one hand, I would proudly say to people, "I have a credit card and I just use it and then my husband pays it off. I don't have to worry about where the money comes from." With the same breath, I would complain about how he "is hiding money from me" and would not tell me anything about the inflow or outflow of our money. "I don't know what he does with the money," I would say, as though it was some big secret.

Little did everyone know, but I did not start asking questions about where our money was needed until we were at the end of our relationship. Life is intriguing indeed; we don't want to look inside ourselves because it makes us accountable for our actions, and yet that is the very thing that liberates us from our own pseudo-self. This pseudo-self is the false identity we have come to believe about ourselves from other people and our life circumstances.

How many times do we show up to work feeling under the weather? If it happens again and again, do we wonder about it? "Just this one last meeting. Just these last touches on this report. Just one more tweak on this presentation." And the best yet, "I will go home right after I do (fill in the blank)."

At home, I found myself doing things around the house even when I knew I did not feel well. "I will just put in one load of laundry. I will just get the dishes into the dishwasher. I will just do this one quick chore to make my day easier tomorrow."

Have you noticed there is always just one more thing before you can rest?

Why Stay in Miserable Situations?

You must be wondering why I stayed in these miserable situations, and believe me, I used to wonder that about other people too. It was never about me. Oh no. I would hear stories about physical abuse, alcoholism, betrayal in relationships and think to myself, "Why do these woman stay? Just leave."

Well, little did I realize that "just leave" was being reflected back at me. I was not happy, so why didn't I just leave? The answer was morbidly simple—I didn't leave because I didn't want to let people down and I lacked the courage in that moment to make any moves that made me uncomfortable. The perception that my family had created around me and would often say to me was that I was being unappreciative of having such a great job when many others did not even have jobs. Not only did I stay at my work because of this strange level of obligation, but I also stayed because I was not ready to answer questions about how I was crazy because I was trying to follow a dream that "would never manifest."

Health, wealth, marriage, career. Each segment of my life had one pattern running through it at the very same time, and that was, I was in paralysis. I actually believed that there was no way out and that more than likely, my entire life would play out exactly this same way.

Exercise—Small Shifts Create Big Impact

When you are in a place of thinking you are paralyzed by life or work choices, the smallest changes in your life can have big impacts. Each small step is a milestone into the next step, which then leads to being comfortable, because you are not changing everything at the same time. It also gives you time to adjust to a new way of being but in a gentler way. We sometimes can feel overwhelmed by changes in our life that seem impossible; therefore, taking small steps makes it easier.

To start you off easily, try implementing these very simple yet profound steps in your work week.

When you start a meeting, take the first ten minutes to connect. Ask each member to describe what's new in his or her life that they would like to share. This allows for some settling-in time before you start on content. Sometimes, sharing a little bit about yourself goes a long way in building relationships.

When booking meetings, have a company policy around how much time there should be between one meeting and the next; stick to that policy. Having a uniform approach makes the life of an administrative assistant much easier. My general approach was thirty minutes between meetings, no meetings during lunch hours, and no meetings after 4:40 p.m.

Have a regular quarterly quality-improvement meeting with a group of people preselected from the entire organization, regardless of their role. You never know where a quality-improvement idea that can save you time, money, and resources will come from. This makes people feel involved in efficiency ideas and feeling they are a part of the organization as a whole. Value your people and they will value you.

Exercise—How to Move from Your Reality to What You Desire

List five things that you feel would make your life full of vitality and abundance.

1 _____
2 _____
3 _____
4 _____
5 _____

List one reason why each of these five things is important to you.

1 _____
2 _____
3 _____
4 _____
5 _____

What is one stepping stone for each thing you want that you are willing to take action on today to get you there?

1 _____
2 _____
3 _____
4 _____
5 _____

Take a moment to reflect on where you do or do not accept that your current reality is exactly as it should be for now. Journal your process.

Chapter 5 Blame Others for the Circumstances of Our Reality

Blaming others for our own misery is so easy. Not only is it easy, we actually whole-heartedly and genuinely believe it is due to no fault of our own that we are unhappy. We blame situations, circumstances, people, God, destiny, and anything else we can point a finger at, and sometimes we can just blame the weather if nothing else is available. "It's too hot for me to think. It's too cold for my bones. The rain wrecked my hair." Sound familiar? We search for things external to ourselves that are responsible for our life.

Let us take something as simple as taking a sip of a hot drink and burning our tongue. Generally, what one may say is something like, "Ouch, I burned my tongue with that hot tea." We don't usually say, "I was silly taking a sip of hot tea and burning my tongue." Or let's take an example of a meeting that was not productive in our eyes and a waste of time. We say, "That meeting was horrible; what a waste of time," rather than "I didn't really say what I needed to say. Instead, I went quiet and hoped someone else would say it."

I could give you many examples of this from my life, because I used to be a master at this blame game. It's a fascinating game indeed we play with ourselves to ensure that we are not held accountable for our current reality and we don't have to take responsibility. It is easy not to look at our own behavior and the choices we make to be where we are. We may even feel

71

that some of those choices were even beyond our control. The reality still is that you have choice, right now, right here, in this exact moment, to change.

Blaming others gives us the false perception that we are helping ourselves. "It's not my fault that my husband is a jerk." "It's not my fault that my manager does not know how to lead." "It's not my fault the client gets angry." "It's not my fault that my colleague is an idiot." The list could literally go around the earth's circumference a few times over. I have blamed anyone I could throughout my life just to take the attention off myself, so that I can bathe in the eternal bliss of victimhood.

Blaming My Parents for Sending Me to India

I had blamed my parents for sending me and my sister to India and leaving us in boarding school. I did not want to understand why they made that choice. I just knew that I blamed them for doing it. I would blame my mother for my feelings of vulnerability when I recalled stories of getting my period for the first time and not having her there. I used to think "If I was with my mom, would this be different?" when I had to get my training bra with my aunt instead of my mom, when I got sick and had to lie down in the dorm. I really missed the compassion and caring we get from our mothers, and often I would imagine her being there with me.

One summer, my parents were coming to visit us in India. I really wanted to get my nose pierced and I knew they would not allow it. I was so determined that I asked one of the girls in the dorm to do it with a needle and thread. I then went on to blame it on the girl who did it, saying that it was done under peer pressure. There are examples of this type of behavior in our lives when we desperately want something to be exactly the way we want it but we don't want to deal with the consequences. Do you recall doing something in your life when you didn't want to be responsible for the consequences, so you found it very easy to blame someone else?

Television Show *Winds of Change*

Sometimes due to our life's circumstances, we get into a place of thinking really small rather than dreaming the big dream for our life. In 2009, when I was filming a television show I called *Winds of Change*, I used to think it was my biggest dream ever. One of the guests on the show—a woman who was going to talk about soul contracts and what we are here to do—asked me to write down what my biggest dream was. Even though her question was very open and I could have thought of anything, I responded with, "To make the show a success." What a beautiful example of thinking small. And yet I did not even know I was thinking small; it seemed like a really big dream to me. This very woman would become my spiritual mentor over the next few years.

It has taken me years to see clearly why that was not my biggest dream. Today, I realize that impacting billions of people positively in the workplace is my biggest dream, to show them that we have choices and we don't have to be miserable at work. Now, that's what I call a dreamer's big dream.

During the filming of *Winds of Change*, my life was at its toughest, with my career in question, my marriage in question, and everything I knew about myself being no longer true. I had come to realize that I was not living my truth. No wonder I could not think big—I was wrapped up in day-to-day problems and challenges, which did not allow me to think past everyday life.

Behind the Camera

When I started doing the television show, my brother and sister were right there by my side, each encouraging me to fulfill my dream. They were there every step of the way with their guidance, support and, above all, their time. There were many aspects of the show in which I found myself not listening, and I ended up losing money because I was not listening to my brother and sister.

There was also one fatal mistake I made that I regret to this day. After the show had aired, I was interviewed by a journalist about my journey in regard to the show. It so happened that at exactly the same time, I was contemplating divorce. I thought if I gave my husband some credit in the interview, even though he did not support my decision in doing the show, he would come around to see how important it was to me. In this interview I forgot to mention the very people who actually stood by me and really made the show possible. My brother relentlessly put in hours and hours of work producing the show; my sister put in hours doing the background operations; my family gave up their home so that we had somewhere to film. I was so stuck in my own web of dealing with my personal issues that I had forgotten my family who had stood by me. It is at times like this when I wish I could turn back the clock and fix the omission. But we can only carry our lessons forward.

I gained a wealth of information filming fifty-two episodes with a hundred and four guests, each bringing their own take on what they felt corporate spirituality meant to them.

When the show finished airing, I would often complain that it had not made any money and that I had put my life savings into the show without any results. I regretted my decision to follow my heart and I regretted all the effort I had put into the show. I had started blaming the channel for charging us too much to air the show; I blamed the industry for adding ad-free television; I blamed myself for not having the money to continue; I blamed corporations that were not willing to sign on as advertisers.

What was wrong in all this was that I was not seeing what I had gained, and rather was focusing on all the things that had not gone well. I had siblings who were willing to stand by me and have faith in me to the point that they dedicated an entire year to the program and wanted nothing in return. I had a team of high-caliber people who wanted nothing more than to do what was in my best interest and share in my success, from the production team to each individual member who wanted to make the show the best it could be.

I had to start looking at this show through another lens, a lens in which the gains would become apparent. We may not have made money per se, but we gained so much more, such as industry credibility and workplace reputation. We learned from some very intellectual and spiritual guests and we formed beautiful relationships that lasted well past the show itself. We learned so much from the experience about the world of television and how the logistics work. The gains well surpassed any financial return on investment, but at first I could not see it that way because I was too busy blaming.

Each situation in our life is a milestone for something else, and the show definitely was that milestone for many things to manifest over the years.

At the time we were filming the show, I was still working full time in that environment with a toxic culture. So, Monday to Friday I would work in a toxic environment and then come home to a weekend of filming some wonderful guests talking about corporate spirituality. Unbeknown to me, I had become a part of that toxic culture, but I could put on a great facade while filming the show. I had become a master at living a dual life.

In the workplace, I would often complain about our working conditions and our management, or the lack thereof. I would complain about how overworked and underpaid we were. I would complain about how long it took to get things approved. Then I realized I was a part of the toxicity. That was a hard mirror to look into, as I didn't like what I saw—the behavior of others—staring right back at me.

Creating a Duality of Blame

I thought my show would be a success and I wouldn't need that job anymore. I had created a huge duality—on one side, I was fulfilling my dream, and on the other side, I was miserable and blaming my misery on anything in sight. It's no joke; they say your external environment reflects how you feel on the inside. The show had become my escape plan. If only I could ensure its success, I would not have to work in that miserable environment, or so I thought. Little did I know that I was the constant in my miserable life and that no success was going to fix that for me. Running away from something is not the answer. But I didn't know better. I was too focused on creating my future without enjoying the present.

At exactly the same time, my husband had become an easy target for blame for my lack of knowledge around our finances. Each time he recommended something, I would get angry because it felt as though he was trying to control me. As a matter of fact, I think there were times when I actually agreed with him and yet, in spite, I still rebelled and probably made some bad financial decisions just out of pure rebellion. "Who is he to tell me how to run my business? He doesn't know what kind of quality is needed for this type of work." And to make matters worse, I did not trust his professional judgment.

My manager at work had also become an easy target for blame for my work environment, as "she does not understand me; she is working against me; she doesn't like me; she is out to get me."

So many people to blame and so little time. What was I to do!

Having a Chest Infection and Working Anyway

Many years ago, I was getting ready to go to work, and yet it had been days since I had felt well. It was a Friday, and I knew I had just a few emails to do and then I could return home and rest for sure. As I arrived at the office, I felt a slight fever coming on. "Just a few hours," I promised myself. I made it to my desk feeling a bit light-headed but "nothing that some tea and throat lozenges can't fix." I was ready to work. Somewhere inside, I knew that most likely it would be another day ending at five o'clock and I was totally fooling myself into believing I was there for a few emails. As I started to write the emails, I found myself concentrating very hard to keep two words together.

A colleague happened to walk into the office, and as she came closer to me she asked, "What is that smell?" When she asked, "Jivi, are you okay? You do not look well at all," I was taken by surprise, as I thought I was doing a very good job of applying makeup and hiding being unwell. Having a nursing background, she knew the smell was of an infection gone very wrong.

I remember looking at her and saying, "I have a bit of a chest infection, but I just need to get this email done and I will head home."

She looked at me and said, "For your sake and the sake of everyone in this office, you need to go now." She walked over to our manager's office and soon enough they were both in my office, having called my husband to pick me up and take me off to the hospital.

I arrived at the hospital feeling fairly incoherent, and I remember being whisked away on a stretcher. I awoke fourteen hours later with a bunch of tubes hanging out of me, a high fever, body shakes, and still very incoherent. I vaguely remember the next two or three days, but I do not recall some of the conversations that transpired. The so-called chest infection had become pneumonia, and from there my body had gone into septic shock. I found myself at home battling this infection for the next two months, unable to move from the bed, which gave me lots of time to think.

I was contemplating, for the first time, when I was going to take my health seriously. In the last year alone, I had been diagnosed with diabetes, high blood pressure, and neuropathy, a condition with a symptom of nerve pain. It was as though my body was crying out to me more and more loudly each time and I did not have my listening ears on. What would make me not want to pay attention to my health and make my work a priority over myself"?

Part of this was my upbringing, as well as having the perception that self-care is being selfish. I could hear my boarding school warden saying, "You're not sick enough to stay home, so go to school." Or I would observe my parents going to work at all costs; whether they were sick or not, they had to work. We grow up with these beliefs that we think are in our best interest. It's as though, if we work hard and survive being at work while we're sick, we'll get some kind of courage award. When I think about what I was putting at stake that day by staying to write that last email, I recognize it was my life. So, why had my life come to this, where I was willing to stake my wellbeing for work?

I will share with you that on the day I went to work sick and this situation happened, I was totally oblivious of my actions. If someone had told me, "Jivi, if you go to work today being this sick, you have a high chance of losing your life," I would have made a different choice. So, what made me unable to say this to myself? Many factors: not wanting to be home, wanting to prove that I too could be at work even when I was sick, not wanting people to think badly of me and my lack of responsibility toward my work, and not wanting to let people down. How foolish, you may think, and yet we do the same sort of thing every day. We put our self-care aside to do things out of obligation and responsibility at the cost of ourselves.

Blissful Workplace

Later, after being in some work environments where I had overcommitted myself, I vowed to not feel that level of obligation to anyone ever again and rather to treat my work environment as an equal exchange. My work would provide me with a paycheck and, in exchange, I would provide my workplace with my experience and skills. This one simple mind shift gave me six years of a blissful workplace.

I also committed to never shying away from conflict, to speaking my truth, to being authentically who I am, and to approaching my work through the lens of humbleness, authenticity, and compassion. I committed to gaining the skills needed to uphold these commitments to myself.

The conflict resolution program not only taught me conflict skills but also how to communicate effectively. Sometimes, the changes we need to make are so simple. If I did not know how to handle conflict, then get some training. How simple! Later, during the course of this program, our instructor told me that I had a beautiful gift in handling conflict and I would do very well as a high-stakes mediator and negotiator. In a matter of months, I went from not liking conflict at all to receiving this type of feedback. It's no joke when they say "What you run from the most is what seeks you the most."

But I'm getting ahead of myself. Let me tell you more of how I got to that blissful workplace.

My Aha Moment

Sometime after recovering from being hospitalized for septic shock, I sat in my office in a miserable mental space, still wondering "What's next?" It was about fifteen years ago, in 2000. I had been complaining about everything for many months without even noticing how I was impacting the people around me. My complaints ranged from how the program was run, to how the manager did not know what she was doing, to how much I really did not like my job, to how other people were underperforming, to how I was being asked to do Excel spreadsheets and strategic plans. Anything you can name, I had a complaint about it.

As a matter of fact, I remember feeling as though there was a huge target on my forehead and my manager was out to get me. I now recognize my wonderful shadow side was showing up to work. You know, that side that you are not really very proud of, but every so often she rears her head and acts in a way that is "not really me." And believe me, I didn't start out this way at the beginning of my career—not at all. As a matter of fact, I was a keener, a people pleaser, so I would do anything that was asked of me. I was respectful and professional and would spend endless hours at work.

As I sat there in that office, which I shared with two other colleagues in 2000, I was venting about something or other as usual and then came the most pivotal moment in my career. For the hundredth time, I said, "I really need to find another job. I just can't take this anymore."

My colleague who is also my friend responded, "Jivi, shit or get off the pot. You are miserable and you are making everyone else around you miserable as well."

I felt a hammer coming down on my heart, and in that exact moment I actually realized how miserable I was. That was my aha moment!

In a strange kind of way, it felt like a relief that it was out in the open, and I felt a lightness in my heart that I had not felt in years. I sighed a big sigh, gathered my belongings, and went home, with the plan that I would resign from my job.

As I drove home, I was in a very strange place of sadness, relief, and disbelief, but then panic set in. "How am I going to tell my family I am leaving a government job where I'm making good money with full benefits and a pension, and I don't have a plan?" "Good grief, are you crazy?" is exactly what I anticipated, and that is exactly the reaction I received. This was the start of me rewriting my story with my destiny pen. I was finally back in the control seat and being accountable for what my life had become.

I Quit My Job and Stayed Home for Six Months

The day my coworker said "Shit or get off the pot" was the day when I found the courage to quit my job and stay home for six months. I call those my "Jerry Springer Days." This is when I lay on the couch in a depression, watching The *Jerry Springer Show* and thinking, "Okay, my life is good. It's not as bad as what they are talking about!" Yes, my life had come down to comparing myself with the guests on *Jerry Springer*, but in all fairness, they made me feel *kinda* normal.

My children were in elementary school then, and they would come home after school day after day to find me still in my pajamas, lying on the same couch. Then one day I remember asking myself, "Did I brush my teeth today?"

I Know What I Don't Want

It was another milestone moment and an almost out-of-body experience. I looked down at myself and watched myself question what my life had become. It was at that pivotal moment that I grabbed a piece of paper. I knew exactly what I did not want in a job. "So," I rationalized, "if I know what I do not want, the direct opposite would be what I do want in a job, right?"

So I began writing my I-do-not-want list on this paper. I did not want to manage people. I did not want to make people feel as though their contribution to the team was worthless. I did not want to do anything with process, structure, and project management. And above all, I did not want anyone around me to feel as though they had lost their authentic voice.

Thoughts on Leadership

I started to imagine my own style of leadership, in which my I-do-not-want list came in very handy, helping me form which characteristics I did want to have as a leader. In the mid-1990s in my work environment, I knew I was different. I handled leadership differently, conflict differently, and my general approach to the work was fun and interactive. My view was that leadership should inspire, motivate, and encourage people to be their best, but not through fear. I loved conflict, as it built the platform for a new relationship to blossom through a new lens, as long as the people involved have the appropriate tools and techniques. Life does not have to be serious all the time; we can accomplish much more through humor and human-to-human connection.

This was not how management saw this at my previous employment. Managers were still stuck in the old style of management—managing through fear, by pushing sales targets, and by repressing uniqueness.

I was a person with a deep yearning to be different. I was not satisfied with the status quo. How do you think I showed up to work? I can tell you exactly. Nothing was ever good enough. I was constantly looking for the next best thing, the next project, the next person to talk to, the next chore to do, the next level of learning I needed to acquire. My life was about "What's next?" instead of being in the moment and enjoying exactly where I was. This constant drive to be in the future was not a happy state for me or anyone around me, because not only did I live this life of "What's next?" but the team I was leading also felt this constant drive to be bigger and better. There is nothing wrong with wanting to be bigger and better, if you also take the time to celebrate the present moment and what you have accomplished in the past.

How many things can you count that you wish you had time for? If you had to take a wild guess at how many people show up to work with a yearning to be something else or be somewhere else, what percentage do you think that would be? As a part of a self-review process I once ran, I asked a team of approximately sixty people if they were happy with their current state, whether at home or at work. Ninety percent of them said no. What does that tell you about how we show up to work? What if I told you there is a way to have a cohesive team in which each person shows up to work as a balanced individual? Would you be willing to commit time and resources?

What Do I Want?

From the list of what I didn't want, I started to build a list of what I did want to do, such as conflict resolution, leadership, team building, facilitation, communication, etc. As I wrote this list of everything that I wanted in a job, I looked at each thing on the list to see how confident I was at that particular skill. From this endeavor began the new me.

Before I knew it, I had enrolled at Royal Roads University in their MBA program at the Justice Institute for conflict resolution training, and I had written to enquire about how to gain my certification in advanced facilitation and business consulting.

The new me all began when I took the first step because my current state had become so miserable that I was willing to act on my desire for something different.

At the time of forming my list, I did not even know that all these activities and trainings combined had a name—Organizational Development Consultant. I just simply knew that was what I wanted to do. When someone told me "That's what OD Consultants do," I remember saying with utter shock, "There is a name for everything I want to do!"

If you truly want to change, you have to be willing to do

something about where you are, even by taking the smallest step forward. It no longer serves you to stay in a miserable or unhappy situation, because you always have a choice. Let me be the first to tell you, you are choosing to be exactly where you are right now, shackled by your own limiting beliefs.

Starting to Do Organizational Development

I remember that when I first started to facilitate organizational-developmental-type work—well before taking my MBA—I would take pieces of Lego and other toys to get a point across at the conferences. When I would tell my father what I was doing, he would say, "Is that what they pay you for? To play games?" To my parents, life was about working hard and being serious, always keeping two jobs so that you could get ahead financially. Therefore, this was the mindset that I had picked up as well, that self-care was being selfish and at no cost should I be leaving work; rather, life was about "toughing it out," even when you were sick or stressed. Even my leader at work would consider simple things like graphics on a PowerPoint silly.

Now, here is the amazing part: the people that I was serving loved the games. There were times in which I had physicians working with Lego to understand patient-physician interaction, writing haiku poetry, and performing skits. At conference after conference, our team was seeing the results of making learning fun. Physicians looked forward to our sessions and, as much as they thought the games were silly, they eagerly took part in them. They could see that something being fun does not take away from its ability to teach us; as a matter of fact, fun enhances the learning experience.

Finding a Perfect Pearl in My MBA Class

I enjoyed my studies because I found that thought leaders on the topic of leadership spoke the same language I did.

It was well into 2007 when one my professors in my MBA class noticed and pointed out that I would not engage in dialogue in a team setting unless I had prepared perfectly structured sentences. I was still not speaking my truth, because I did know how to formulate the sentences. Therefore, it was better to say nothing at all. Probably that was why I had gone along passively with others' decisions, holding resentment deep inside me rather than just saying what I felt.

She started asking me some questions that led to why I was behaving that way and, guess what, it stemmed back to my life story. Each story in our life is a perfect pearl —a lesson that must be lived in that moment in time for us to learn and grow.

Taking Responsibility

If you feel right now that the world is conspiring against you, it's probably because you are conspiring against yourself. If only in all these situations years ago I had taken a moment to take my antagonists' perspectives into consideration. Let's fast-forward a few years to gain a better understanding of the impact of listening better without blaming. First, I had to drop all judgment that people were out to get me and did not have my best interest at heart.

One day, I was cleaning my bathroom cupboards—you know, deep in the cupboard where you have shoved things further and further in, until the day you decide to get right in to clean it. I, in that pivotal moment, realized I had at least twelve bottles of shampoo and an unlimited number of bottles of makeup that

I might never use. Yes, it was that type of cupboard cleaning. As I sat there in front of the cupboard, I realized that cleaning our internal conditioning and mental constructs is very similar to this type of cupboard cleaning: we have to go deep inside ourselves to deconstruct and clean out all our conditioning.

It's at these moments when you realize how much conditioning we actually have around such a simple concept as blaming others. I had learned from society that it was okay to blame the world for my problems. That way I didn't need to take action; I could just find something to blame and complain about. I decided that I was going to clean out my conditioning and take responsibility for each situation that I blamed in my life.

So, there I sat with a journal in hand and I started to mind map each challenge I remembered encountering. In the center of the mind map, I wrote a description of the situation, and then around it I started to make notes about what things were going well in each of those times. As I mind mapped, a pattern started to emerge. This pattern was one of low self-worth, wanting to prove myself to everyone around me, and low self-confidence. This is where I want to point out that doing the inner journey is not easy work. It takes time and effort, and a desire to go inside to process why you do things the way you do them.

Uncovering What Was Holding Me Back

In 2011 when I had moved to Nanaimo post-divorce, I was alone, all alone. As I turned on the lights to all the dark places that I had not had time to think about, there were some things that became very clear. I had lived a life of blaming other people and situations for the series of circumstances in my life and I had not even considered how I had contributed to the reality that I was living. I had not even considered that I was in control of my life and if I wanted to have a different life, it was all based on my choices. So, if I desired a different life, I could make different choices regardless of the consequences. And lastly, I had led my life from a place of fear of what others might think of me. I was always worried about what that person would say or what the other person would do. And yet conveniently, I was forgetting that this was my life and how I chose to live it should be of no concern to others.

All these things combined were holding me back from living the life that I truly wanted to live—one of no drama, which meant no gossip or rumors, no talking about other people or judging them. I wanted a life of serenity and peace, doing the things that I loved to do—a life of freedom and liberation from every role that society was telling me I should be filling. I wanted to live for myself, doing the things that I loved to do.

I started to do a little experiment during this period of reflection. When I attended meetings at work, I would be extra attentive to how people were interacting with me and how I was interacting with them. It's as though during this time of reflection my ability to observe my surroundings was on high definition. I noticed that if something was not going well at work, instead of trying to find something to blame, I was the first to say where I could accept responsibility.

When people noticed me doing this, they felt an openness to discuss their own accountability. The question was, if I was being vulnerable as a leader, could I still maintain a level of respect among the team? Would they perceive my vulnerability as a sign of a weak leader who made mistakes?

Remember the mental conditioning I spoke about earlier; this was all mental conditioning. A leader is supposed to have all the answers. A leader is supposed to act in a certain way. A leader doesn't share her personal life. The list goes on and on. I was breaking all the norms of how a leader should behave. I was being raw, vulnerable, transparent, and authentic. If I was having a crummy day, I would say I was having a crummy day.

Could this authentic approach really work with the team?

Sometimes we like to say we are authentic, and then somehow it just doesn't apply to leadership because there are things we think we can't or shouldn't share with the team. And, of course, there are many things about your personal life you may choose to not share, and yet so many more that you could.

Sometimes there are aspects to your strategic direction that you may not want to share with your team yet, because they may impact them in a negative way. This way the team stays focused on the task at hand. This type of privacy conflict may come up in mergers where information is very delicate and must be released on a need-to-know basis. Another item to keep private might be when there is to be a significant change in leadership or even when someone is terminated from their job. You would maintain privacy so as to not worry the team. In these types of situations, team members appreciate it more when you say something like "I am not privy to share that information just yet," or ask, "What is important to you about knowing that information?" This allows you to address the underlying fear and is much better than saying something like "I don't know." Guess what! Your team knows that you know, so be authentic with them.

On a more personal note, I started to share a little about what I had done on the weekend at our Monday morning virtual watercooler meetings. I did it to see what impact it would have on our culture. The team started to open up about their lives as well.

I started to reach out to our team members for advice on certain plans and strategies, and they responded with greater involvement and creativity. We started to laugh with each other and connect in a way that I had not thought was possible. Still feeling a little sceptical, I moved slowly and pushed the limits each time, and each time the team surprised me with their loyalty, dedication, and creativity. This increased as time went by. I would laugh, be fully engaged in their stories, and would share my past experiences that helped them understand me better. And yet at the same time, I would be comfortable every so often showing emotions such as tears about something that hadn't gone so well. Did this emotion make me a bad leader? Absolutely not. As a matter of fact, people said they loved that I was authentic and could relate to them and their work. They said that because I listened and was willing to be vulnerable, I could comprehend what worked and what did not work for them. As a matter of fact, mutual respect for where each person thrived and survived was growing on our team.

If we continue to blame others, we rob ourselves of the beauty that resides in reflection and in the actions to make things better. Sometimes, the pendulum can also swing the other way and we can blame ourselves for everything without a level of self-forgiveness.

The greatest impact comes from processing, reflecting, and acting. Do something about what you don't like about your life.

Exercise—Holding Up the Mirror

When you tie emotions like blame to a situation or person, those emotions, those situations, and those people are simply reflecting something back to you that you are ready to heal within yourself. Until you are ready to accept that you are a part of the problem, I would recommend not doing this exercise.

In your journal or just on a piece of paper, write down one situation that you would like to do some deep work on to understand your role better.

1. What was it about this situation or person that annoyed, frustrated, hurt, and angered you the most?
2. Now think about a time that YOU may have acted in exactly the same way as the other person.
3. If that person was reflecting something back to you, what would the reflection be asking of you?
4. Ask yourself, "What am I to learn from this reflection and who do I need to reach out to for healing?"

Chapter 6 Look at Life as a Series of Seemingly Unrelated Events

The Dots of Our Life

Why do we wait so long to connect the dots of our life?

Each event in your life is like a pearl in a necklace. Each pearl is divinely guided to happen at an exact moment in time and to come together in one piece of pure elegance. We often don't sit down to fully understand how each event in our life connects the dots to what and who we are today. What if each situation that you encounter is just one piece of the puzzle and one day you will be able to pull all the pieces together to see the full picture?

My journey has been no different from yours in that regard. When I reflect back on everything that has gone on in my life, not only do I realize that each situation occurred in the correct timing sequence, but also each circumstance was meant to happen for me to learn and grow before the next challenge presented itself.

I can think back to the age of seven and follow the series of events in my life and know that if even one event were out of place, my journey would have been completely different and I would be completely different, myself, today. The challenges that presented themselves were so well timed that it was only when I was mature enough to handle the situation that it actually occurred in my life. There are, of course, two different timelines of my personal and professional life; however, they are completely intertwined with each other, from my childhood lessons to how I show up to work each day, even to this day.

I would never have anticipated that the thirty years after starting as a janitor in a medical office in 1992 would unfold in perfect alignment with my professional growth. All I knew at that time was that I was driven and motivated to be the best at whatever I was doing, with a thirst for learning and self-development. My career path was probably where the connection of the dots was the most significant and apparent. Someone who watered plants and cleaned toilets in a medical practice in Vancouver would come to accomplish strategic leadership roles in healthcare and gain an MBA specializing in Leadership from Royal Roads University in 2011 and a PhD in Spiritual Research from the University of Sedona in 2016. Who would have thought that? Not me, yet there it was, a series of events that seemed unexpectedly related.

Grade 9 Boy Loves Me

There was a young boy in Grade 9 at my boarding school in India who fell in love with me. The entire school knew about this, and I, of course, did not give him the time of day. I had quite the ego back then, to say the least. For three years, he quietly wrote me messages and letters, but not once did he come to talk to me. For three years, this one-sided love affair continued, to the point that all the other girls and boys in our class were now judging me for not responding to true love. The boy's love grew more and more profound over the years. I don't have any of his letters now, but he was quite the poet and he loved writing long, creative, romantic sentences.

Chapter 6

Remembering Boy Who Loved Me

When I was going through the worst times in my marriage, I would often think about that boy at boarding school, and I would think how intriguing karma is: I gave no heed to the one who loved me, and now the one I married gave no heed to me. I would think about that boy's letters and the time he took to compose them, scribe them, and somehow send them to me.

There were other girls in the dorm who found him very attractive, and they would often tell me how horrible I was to break his heart all the time and how dedicated his love was to me. They would ask me to break his heart once and for all so they could tell him that they loved him. They would compare his love to Layla Manjun or Heer Ranjha (Indian lovers who died for the sake of their love). Hence, the blame game continued. I even blamed his beautiful love for me as the reason for my misery in my marriage. How is it that we are so great at justifying all of our current reality and associating it with anything we can put our thoughts on?

Leaving Marriage

I sometimes wonder how many people would leave a marriage or workplace if someone told them they would have to heal from emotional pain. What if when you left a marriage there were no broken relationships, no hurt feelings, no negative emotions, no feeling of loss or regret and, above all, happiness? Wouldn't that just be a wonderful world? Probably not. In this perception of so-called happiness, there would be no growth, no learning, no building strength and courage, no new beginnings, and no development as a human being.

Each day, you robotically go to work or do household

responsibilities in the same way that you've done for years. We put off joy, happiness, and bliss, hoping for a time of pleasure that never comes. The same goes for our relationships—we stay in relationships and sometimes can go an entire lifetime maintaining them even though we know we are miserable. So, what makes us go to work each day and be in unhappy relationships even when we know they do not serve our soul purpose? We forget that we hold the pen to our own story; we forget that we have the ability to rewrite, edit, delete, or, better yet, write a new story for our life. We conveniently forget that the way our lives are right now is because choices we made in the past are now manifesting in our present.

Where Shall I Live?

When I went through my divorce many years back, I remember having to consider where I would move geographically. This may seem silly to some, but if you marry straight out of Grade 12, have only known one man as a life partner, have lived a very sheltered life, and have two children to consider, where you are going to move becomes a major life decision.

I considered Nanaimo a beautiful city. I visited it frequently as part of my job, and every time I drove through the town I would think what a great place it would be to live. When it came time to deciding where to move, I chose to move from Vancouver across the Georgia Strait to the city of Nanaimo on Vancouver Island. Many people have asked me why Nanaimo, and my answer is simple: "This is where my heart wanted to be, and I was finally listening to my heart."

I recall the very long drive from the house to the ferry terminal; it felt almost surreal that I was moving out. When I think back, it was as though someone else's movie was running in the background. My best friend was there by my side, and in each moment she was trying to ensure that I was okay.

In my mind I kept questioning, "Is this really happening? What was I thinking? Am I crazy to leave my family after twenty years? Is this really happening to me?"

So many thoughts and such little time.

When our two-hour ferry ride came to an end, it was evening. We headed to my new condo and moved in our belongings—mostly mine—from the car. We decided we should get a bite to eat. As we sat down at the restaurant, I ordered a Caesar salad. I sat there staring at it, thinking, "I should probably go back. I've made a big mistake."

I looked up at my friend and said, "I think I need to go back."

Just to provide some context here, we had just finished moving fifteen large boxes up fourteen flights of stairs into my new apartment on the fourteenth floor. She looked up at me from her plate of food and, with very kind eyes, asked, "Can we finish our food and then go?"

Not the response I was thinking I would get. I was ready for her to say, "Are you crazy? We just lugged all those things upstairs!" I was ready for a fight. I had it all planned out in my head as to what I was going to say to make it perfectly okay for me to go back.

But her response made my entire fight rather anticlimactic.

We finished our food and before I knew it, we had decided to pick up some things for the condo, like dishes, bedding, and small things, still with the plan that we were going back in the morning, because the last ferry had already left for the evening.

When my friend asked what my greatest fears were, I said, "Paying the bills and getting stuck in the elevator."

How silly that at that time those were my most greatest

fears. So, what did my friend do? When we were back at the condo, she stopped the elevator as though we were stuck and called the emergency number listed in the elevator to see what would happen. As we heard the voice on the other side asking if we were okay, she responded by saying it was an accident. After hanging up, she looked at me. "Now you know what to do if you're stuck!

"Take a shower and let's go to bed. We have an early rise tomorrow to pack everything back up."

As I stood in the shower, crying and watching the water roll down the drain, I realized that the old Jivi was washing down the drain and a new Jivi would emerge with time. It was time for me to heal myself. I walked out into the bedroom and lay on the bed in the fetal position, wondering what would happen next. That night was probably the hardest night of my life. Crying, I fell asleep well into the morning. I awoke to my friend covering me with a soft blanket she had bought.

"Believe me, you will need this," she had said when we had been buying some odds and ends the night before.

That blanket became my saving grace. I felt its beautiful softness every night as I cried into it many, many nights. So, the following morning we woke up and I decided that we would leave everything where it was and I would go back to see how things were at home. In my mind I thought, "If the kids are not well, I will just return to Nanaimo, pick up my stuff, and move back. That sounds like an easy plan, right?"

Well, when I got back home, the kids were in great shape—they were happy and were looking forward to visiting me each weekend. So, I had no more excuses. I quickly turned around and left my marital home, this time for good.

This time I made the two-hour ferry ride to Nanaimo to an empty condo on my own. I was not sure how I was going

Chapter 6

to handle all that, but I knew somewhere in my heart that all would be well. "One day at a time, one day at a time," I kept repeating to myself. As I turned the key in the door to my condo, I was also turning the key to my new self.

My friend had left me a beautiful journal and written, "Make this journal your best friend."

Over the next few days, as I was overcome with emotions and started to have panic attacks, I would take out my journal and begin to pour my heart out.

After a year of joining me each weekend in my condo, my children decided to move to Nanaimo as well, and there began our search for our new home. It took us about six months to find the perfect place, and as excited as we all were, we were all scared as well. It would be my first major purchase on my own, and arranging all the finances and paperwork for the mortgage would definitely be a life-learning experience. When I went to arrange the mortgage, the bank representative looked at me and said, "You have hardly any assets and no liabilities." My credit card was always a secondary card to my husband's. "So basically, you don't have any financial ground to stand on to get a mortgage." I remember looking at her with my eyes filling up with tears, feeling the helplessness that everyone had warned me about. "Maybe they are all right," I thought. "Maybe I can't make it on my own."

This is when things got interesting. Instead of taking her words verbatim and accepting defeat, I went to work on some creative problem-solving. Before I knew it, there I was in the bank, signing the approval letter for my mortgage.

My Friend Had Been Helping Me right after Her Surgery

Sometimes as we get to the far side of a situation I call "life paralysis," we realize something. In 2014 I was reflecting on my journey over the past few years, and I came to the shocking realization that when I moved to Vancouver Island and my friend helped me move, she had just had breast cancer surgery a few weeks earlier. Not only did she help me pack my things from our Vancouver home, but she helped me lift everything, put the boxes in my car, and unload everything into my new condo. There were about twenty or more boxes, many heavy with books.

When I had this realization two years after moving, I just sat there in self-criticism, wondering how I could not have considered my friend in the moment. How did I forget that she had had major surgery and there she was, carrying each of my boxes up and down stairs? For two years she had never mentioned a thing. I was in utter disbelief that I could have missed something so crucial. After a few hours of feeling embarrassed, ashamed, and guilty, I gave her a call. There was absolutely no way that I could think of to say sorry that could make this any better. I started out the call with something like "I was just sitting here, thinking about my move post-divorce, and I came to a realization that I am very ashamed about. I didn't even think about you and that you had had major surgery just weeks before." Before I continued to stumble over my words, attempting to say sorry in my guilt-filled way, she stopped me and said, "It's done. You needed me and I wanted to be there for you; that's all that matters."

This one situation taught me so much about how selfish we can sometimes be without even knowing it, and how critical it is to have friends who support you no matter what. I also learned how unselfish some people can be when they are giving and caring.

Later in life, I came to learn that I could break free from feeling paralyzed, simply by dancing with the storm and embracing its power.

Becoming Financially Knowledgeable Post-Divorce

When you look at yourself, it's hard to accept that you are behaving in a way that is not in alignment with what you actually want or desire. To top it off, you might be thinking your problems are everyone else's fault.

When I first moved out of my home post-divorce, I blamed so much of my lack of financial knowledge on my husband. My thoughts included "He is hiding money from me," "I don't know what he's done with our money," "He wants to wring me out of all the money and keep it for himself," and "He is greedy and is keeping money aside." The reality was very different. I had made a choice to be uninvolved in our finances. I wanted life to be easy so that I didn't have to be realistic about what we earned and what we spent.

Realizing I had made a choice to be uninvolved financially was a hard lesson to learn, and yet an important part of my growth and development as a whole person could only happen once I recognize my position.

Now, you may wonder what I learned by taking financial accountability. I got to know and understand my financial situation and how to stay on top of it so that my money works for me. I even mind mapped a journal entry on the value of a dollar for me. The question I asked myself was "What does a dollar mean to me?" I concluded that the value of a dollar is all about what it allows me to do in relation to traveling, giving to charity, and doing humanitarian work—nothing more and nothing less.

Why Do We Want to Work?

Work environments are no different from home environments in the sense that the business must work from a budget perspective and that we are accountable for gaining the knowledge of how budgeting works. We are there to make money and possibly satisfy an internal passion about something we love to do. How many of us actually love the work we do? This may come as a surprise to you, but believe me when I say, not that many. We are so busy finding fault in others and blaming them that we may not recognize that the real issue is that we are avoiding making a change in our life.

Let me share with you some of the basic conditioning that makes us believe in blame. Think about when you were in elementary school and someone took your pencil. You perhaps blamed others and yet very often you would find your pencil either on the ground or in your desk. We complained about bad grades, saying, "The teacher is horrible" or "The teacher doesn't like me." We learned to blame other kids who were not sharing their toys, when the reality was that we sometimes just wanted our own way. This is no different from being at work and blaming things on our leaders or coworkers. If I did not meet the goals at work, I might say it was because "I did not get the go-ahead fast enough" or "I did not have the appropriate resources" or "too many changes were happening" or "someone was not pulling their weight." And then of course when something goes wrong, "I knew it right from the beginning." You can see how deep the conditioning for blame is, even when there is fear of consequences. At what point in our life do we stand back and first reflect on what our role was in the situation and where we are accountable? We are accustomed to first blaming others, then maybe we will consider looking at ourselves.

Fear is an interesting emotion when it comes to pointing a finger. We are sometimes scared of the consequences, scared of hurting someone's feelings, and scared that we might be held responsible. So, if there were no fear, would there be less blame?

In our workplace, we fostered a safe environment by holding off-the-record meetings each month. Usually, we encouraged open dialogue in a very flat organization, so we were comfortable with putting all our thoughts on the table. We called these our "put the moose on the table" conversations. However, the off-the-record meetings were exactly that. If you don't know what your team is really thinking, how can you best provide learning and development?

In the off-the-record meetings, we were all ears to what people were experiencing in the field, listening to what was being said and what was not being said. We then took all that information and built our training programs around what we had heard; no individual was reprimanded for what they said or shared. We replaced fear with respect. When fear is absent, we can gain authenticity and open conversation. Each meeting was carefully planned and executed with purpose and outcomes.

Each year we would send out a list of all the meetings we had had over the year, and each person had an opportunity to say which ones had worked and which ones we didn't need the next year. Again, we were giving the team control and accountability so that when they attended a meeting, it was one that the majority agreed was needed. This way no one could blame anyone else for wasting their time. There were many weekly opportunities within safe environments to voice any concerns that people were having.

Considering Jumping in Nanaimo

Some very significant milestones occurred the year after my divorce, milestones that taught me many life lessons. The most significant lessons were learning to live in solitude and healing from the inside. I don't think I really understood how loud silence can be until I moved from a full house to being on my own for the first time in forty-three years. The silence was deafening at times, as I could even hear the soft throbbing of my heartbeat in my ears. Sometimes I did not know which was worse: the emptiness in my heart or the constant silence around me.

As Christmas came near that year, I stood on the sundeck of my fourteenth-floor apartment wondering, "If I jump, will I die before I hit the water below or will I still be conscious?" I felt anything had to be better than what I was feeling. Right at that pivotal moment, my phone rang and it was my dearest friend. "How are you doing?" she asked.

"Just fine" was my answer. "Just fine."

Little did she know what I was thinking just minutes before the call.

My kids also kept me going. Each Friday I would pick them up from the mainland and take them to Nanaimo to spend the weekend with me. Then each Sunday I would drop them off. The countdown began again each Monday; each and every day thereafter, I would eagerly await the upcoming Friday. Every Sunday I would make the quiet two-hour ferry ride back to Nanaimo on my own, having dropped them off. This cycle continued for one year.

Each time, I wondered when my journey would end. "The journey" refers not just to these ferry rides back and forth, but to my healing from the inside.

Diabetes and Hypertension and later Neuropathy

When I was diagnosed in 1998 with diabetes and hypertension, soon to be followed by a diagnosis of neuropathy, I had no choice but to pay attention, because I was now in a level of pain that I could neither ignore nor control. Had all these circumstances not happened, I would not have researched alternative means of healing. I might not have discovered the benefits of yoga or of practicing Ayurveda or even of understanding the disease cycle from a non-medicinal perspective. If I had not received all these diagnoses, I could not have used myself as an example of someone who manages her chronic pain through the art of mindfulness.

My credibility once again was based on personal experience. When speaking to a physician, I could share my own experience of staying off medication and being able to control my own pain levels through meditative practice. Just like being a janitor in a medical practice was a significant part of my credibility in healthcare, my own medical issues built my credibility for my corporate mindfulness program.

Everything that I am sharing with you takes time to process. I have said this before and will say it again: it is not easy to process, reflect, and change the way we behave. However, it does become much easier as we continue to refine our skills. For example, nowadays I can remember a particular situation, quickly process its meaning, take the lessons I've learned from it, and link them to the next step of my life.

Masters of Crafting Our World

We are masters of crafting a world around us that others may perceive as perfect and seamless. How often I used to hear "You are so lucky. You have the perfect husband, the perfect family, the perfect job. You have your life made." Little did everyone know how broken up I was inside and feeling stuck because of all the choices I had made in my life.

At some point, I had even lost touch with whose life I was actually living, the life I desired or the one that people wanted me to live so I could uphold their ideal for my life. This costume we wear for other people eventually becomes the exact thing that paralyzes us and makes us feel as though we are exploding inside and yet have no clue why.

My divorce shocked people, because our family had seemed perfect to outsiders: a secure government job, two beautiful children, a home that was almost debt-free, vehicles paid off, and a great marriage. People would say, "Your husband doesn't drink; he doesn't go out; he is so dedicated to his children. You have your life made. What is your problem, Jivi?"

My problem was not what they thought; it was actually that I had not made sense of my entire life. If you could imagine a stage play being performed in which the main character is saying lines that actually belong to other characters, that is how I felt. I was a character in a stage play who had no lines of my own. I had never sat down to determine what I wanted from life, what my likes and dislikes were, what a good day looked like for me, how I wanted to live my life. I had never considered myself. When I started to put all the pieces of my life together, all the beautiful things that had occurred and all the things that had gone horribly wrong, there were some clear patterns of my own behavior that I needed to look at and change.

So, where do you begin to make sense of your life? I'm glad you asked, because here are some steps to help you begin your journey. Remember to be gentle with yourself during the process.

Exercise—Finding the Overlapping Patterns

1. On a blank piece of paper, create two timelines, one personal and one professional. Begin to document in short sentences some of the milestones that stand out for you along these timelines.
2. On your professional timeline, think back to your very first job and how that job impacted you. See if you can draw any alignments from the transferable skills you learned at your first job to the way you are today.
3. On your personal timeline, think back to your childhood. What do you remember the most about how you got along with others? Can you identify the top five stories from your youth that you find yourself sharing over and over again with others?
4. In each story, what made you emotional? When do you remember crying or laughing the most? In your work environment, where did you find the most joy and where did you really struggle?
5. Once you have created these timelines, draw out some patterns that you see emerging. Are there overlaps between the patterns of your personal and professional timelines? You will see that the work patterns will inevitably have points of interception with your personal life.

Chapter 7 Not Willing to Go through the Pain of Healing

Why Is Pain a Part of Healing?

Healing from situations in our life is a difficult journey; don't let anyone tell you otherwise. There are many layers to healing, and they take time and sometimes even repetitive actions to deal with the same situation. Just when you think you are done with an issue, it hits you again through a different trigger and you find yourself sobbing over the same situation once again.

Probably why many of us choose not to look inside the dark closets of our memories for many years is because we know we may cry, feel sad, disappointed, regretful, angry, and worse yet, we might lose control of ourselves and our emotions. Some of us may even believe we don't need to look at past issues because they don't impact us. Others may ask themselves, "Why should I dig up old graves when I am very happy in my present life?"

If we bring up something for healing, then we have to face it, acknowledge it, and even be accountable for some or all parts of it. This is what is actually difficult. It is not the healing itself that is difficult; rather, it is the accountability for when we have to look at ourself as being a part of the issue.

The healing process has become integral to who I am as a person, and each day I make a new commitment to myself to bring up things I have buried deeply so that I can face them, embrace them, and create an action plan to move forward from all that dormant energy.

Many years ago, I remember having a special dream. I can recall it vividly to this day, even though I did not write it down anywhere. In my dream, I entered an elevator that felt really dark, musky, and gloomy. It started to go down, and we went down for a really long time. I say "we" because there were others in this elevator with me, including a little wee man who seemed to be in charge. When the elevator doors finally opened, we were in a dark place covered with graves. There was earth everywhere. Some graves were open and some were closed.

We were each directed to a particular grave, and I stood in front of the one I was directed to in complete and utter shock and disbelief. "Where am I?" I thought. "Is this the underworld? Am I dead?" It was a dark, dark place that reflected death. To this day, when I recall this dream I hold my stomach, as being there gave me a bad feeling.

The little wee man handed me a shovel and walked away. As I looked around, people who had been on the elevator with me started to dig into the grave in front of them. I started to do the same. During the digging, I was sweating and exhausted, and at one point I sat down beside the grave and broke down crying. The shovel was getting heavier and heavier, and I was becoming more and more exhausted. I could not understand at all what I was doing there or what this was accomplishing.

As I sat there feeling tired and with a sadness coming over me, I looked up and saw everyone else had started to walk toward the elevator, so I followed. "We are going back. Thank goodness," I thought.

When we entered the elevator, it was brighter than before and I could almost see all the faces of the other people. Everyone seemed tired, and yet there was a sense of relief on their faces. We had surrendered at some point during the digging without really knowing what was going on.

When the elevator opened this time, we were faced with magnificent greenery that went off into infinity. I had never seen the myriad of shapes and colors of such flowers before. I smelled the most beautiful aroma of pure sweetness. What a contrast to what I had just seen below!

If you haven't guessed it already, I will tell you that my dream was about digging up the entire gunk that I had buried deep, deep down inside myself. The truths that I did not want to face were now right in front of me to dig up and heal. It was time and I was ready. To give you some perspective, this dream came to me when I had just divorced and moved to Vancouver Island in 2010. The next six years were filled with lots of digging and then coming up for air in the beauty of the greenery. Each time I dug into the dark corners of my soul, I would remind myself that there would be beauty at the end of all the processing and reflecting I was doing.

Each situation that impacts our lives in a negative way requires healing, and the healing process is very intriguing indeed. We heal in each moment in time only the level that can be healed in that particular moment. This is why many of us find ourselves asking, "Why is this situation coming back now? I thought I had done the work and healed this part of me."

Over the coming years, I became accustomed to many different modalities of healing, including mental modalities such as coaching and counseling; spiritual ones such as prayer and meditation; and physical healing such as Chakradance, Yoga, and craniosacral therapy.

One time, I mentioned to a friend that I really wanted to join a sweat lodge. She was attending one that month and asked me if I would like to join. Reluctantly, I said yes. This is what happens, right? We say we want to do something and then someone says here is a way to do it, and then we get scared because we are not expecting someone to present us with the option.

She and I arrived the morning of the sweat and she introduced me to the gentlemen who would be holding space for us during the sweat itself. My friend told him that I was scared because I was claustrophobic, so I would need some additional support. He was amazingly understanding and guided me to sit between my friend and his wife so that I felt safe.

Once all the preparations were complete and we had been cleansed, he asked me to enter the sweat and to lay some leaves on the ground. Looking back, I realize this was probably to give me some comfort inside the space before everyone else entered, as it gave me something to do.

I was feeling fairly comfortable, as I had seen how much space each person would occupy inside. When people started to enter the sweat lodge, though, it quickly started to fill in. Once the circle got to just over half full, my panic started to set in. Just as when real life gets tough and we simply want to run away rather than face what needs to be faced in our life, I wanted to leave. There were twelve of us in a very small space, sitting knee to knee. You can imagine the heat from the rocks removing all the toxins from our bodies through sweat. I turned to the organizer's wife and said, "May I please leave?"

She responded, "Every time you desire to leave, sit here for an additional sixty seconds and see if the feeling goes away. If it does not, you can leave."

After I sat there for the additional sixty seconds, I felt comfortable again.

As I became slightly more comfortable, I was asked whether

they could close the entrance. When the entrance was closed, it was darker than I had ever known darkness to be. It was blacker than black, no joke, with not a speck of light to be seen. It felt as though my sweat was closing in on me and I could no longer breathe in the heat.

Our mind is such a fascinating thing, as it creates fear sometimes for no reason at all. My heart wanted to stay inside the sweat lodge and my mind was telling me I would die if I did not leave right away. It was a battle of my heart versus my head; that was very evident.

Now, if you have never been in a sweat lodge, let me tell you it highlights every single fear that you may have, in high definition, all in the interest of healing that which is ready and needs to be healed that day. For me, my fear of closed spaces, personal space issues, and darkness were in full gear. "I am going to die," I thought. I was imagining every possible negative thing that could go wrong, and then finally it happened: I surrendered to being there, and that's when the real healing began.

When we surrender to a situation being exactly as it is in that moment and nothing more, healing begins.

There were four rounds of entering the sweat lodge for twenty minutes each time, and for the second round I offered to sit outside; I was honored with being the fire keeper. Here began another layer of healing as I sat outside by myself. I was feeling guilty for not being in the sweat lodge, and I was sitting outside in a forest all by myself. I wondered if they would hear me scream. I thought to myself, "What will I do if I am faced with a bear or a snake? Would they even hear me yell for help?"

I was having many negative thoughts, just as I had inside the sweat lodge. Different circumstances, and yet the emotional response was exactly the same: I was going to die. There was no in-between for me. There was only one option—I would die, either of not breathing inside in the sweat lodge or from an animal outside it. I had no idea how loud a leaf falling in the forest could be when I was fearful, sitting in utter silence by myself in the middle of nowhere.

Then it happened again: I surrendered to my environment outside. "If I die, I die," I thought. All of a sudden, I could hear the frogs singing to each other and the birds chirping. Even the leaves were making a melody as they fell. I felt one with the forest and one with everyone inside the lodge. What a profound shift from death to oneness.

Facing your so-called demons is no easy task. As a matter of fact, it's not for the faint-hearted at all. It takes oodles of courage to sit with yourself and look into all the choices you have made to be exactly where you are today. You are the epitome of your manifestations and you have manifested everything you face right now, the good, the bad, and the ugly. Hard to digest, isn't it, that you, and only you, are responsible for the circumstances you are in right now?

When I thought about all the things that I needed to heal, I felt overwhelmed and I thought the crying would never end. It was difficult to have a side of myself show up that I really didn't like; that was the side of me that I was not really proud of, the side that had betrayed my parents' trust, the side that had lived a life feeling resentment toward my childhood, and the side that felt guilty for leaving a twenty-year marriage. This was the side that I would later come to love.

Healings for the Neuropathy

At this point, the neuropathy in my feet had taken a turn for the worse. I decided to start seeing a chiropractor, hoping there was some way she could reduce the pain in my feet. I wasn't fully aware at that time that our physical symptoms are simply manifestations of our soul crying out for us to listen, and so they show up as physical manifestations.

The chiropractor asked me, "Have you ever had back pain? You have inflammation and a protrusion in your lower back." She called it spondylitis.

My response was, "Not in the past, but recently I have started to experience some minor discomfort." I explained some of my history, about how I had just moved from the mainland and was recently divorced.

She asked me some details surrounding the divorce and then shared something very interesting. She said, "When we are in an unhappy place, we don't recognize the physical pain because we are so worried about our mental state—we don't have time to focus on all the physical things going on in our body. Once we remove ourselves from that state of being and we start to feel safe and secure again, our body starts to relax and all the pain becomes more predominant. Each physical pain comes up for healing, and then we have to deal with it because we can't hide from it anymore."

"Yep," I thought, "I continue to dig up all the things that are buried really deep, pain in my back, pain in my feet, and to be really honest, my entire body is hurting in some way or another." The oddest things would show up as pain. For example, my clavicle would hurt. When have you ever heard someone say, "Oh, I have a sore clavicle!" It felt as though not only was I falling apart mentally and emotionally but also physically. My body was starting to exhibit physical signs of everything emotional that was going on internally.

A Year of Healing

During this entire year of healing, I was still working and each day had to find the motivation to show up to work. Very few people knew about my divorce, as I did not want to have to explain the situation over and over again. I was fortunate enough to have a leader who transferred my work to Nanaimo and I could work virtually from my home. This not only gave me some time to be reclusive, but also saved me from having to dress up each day to go to work. I must say, the entire divorce was divinely guided. Everything seemed to be coming together, except me.

With divorce rates being so high, you are either showing up to work going through this scenario yourself, you know someone who is going through it, or you are working with someone who is going through it. Now, you're probably thinking, "Why is an employee's divorce my concern or business?" Here is why. I showed up to work each day as a whole person. I could not separate my emotions about my divorce from who I was. This meant I was more emotional than usual: I got angry faster, I cried sometimes for no reason, I was not fully present in each conversation and, above all, my mind was occupied with my personal stuff.

Kudos to the best leader I ever had for allowing me to show up at work as a whole person and giving me the openness to be at work or call it a day when I needed to. We rarely talked about my divorce; however, I always knew he was there for me through his little acts of kindness. If we were on a call together and he could sense that I was disengaged, he would step in smoothly so no one knew. He would call me on a Friday afternoon and ask me to take the afternoon to myself. He just allowed me to be the best that I could be on any given day. In return, I was at work every day doing my best and showing appreciation for being allowed some flexibility in my work. Every so often, he would ask, "How's it going? Do you need me to help with anything?"

I would quietly respond, "No, I am doing okay, thank you."

Frankly speaking, I didn't know what anyone could do for me. I had to travel this journey myself, by myself.

Tired of Being Tired

You might wonder why some people don't want to heal themselves. Not only was I rebuilding myself mentally, emotionally, and spiritually, but the next few years involved taking a hard look at my physical situation as well. I questioned whether all this healing and looking into all the dark corners were worth the effort. I asked myself, "What if I just left it? Really, is my recovery really worth the pain and really worth having swollen eyes all the time from crying? Is it not possible for me to not forgive anyone and simply move on in my own life? I don't have to forgive, right?"

I have to say that the crying that regularly happens is very different from the crying of healing. Healing crying is deep grieving and whimpering; it is heavy and exhausting, just like shoveling in my dream. However, once I processed whatever I needed to process, I would feel a relief, a letting go, and a strange relaxation in my chest, much like the infinite greenery in my dream. Then I felt freedom and liberation from the things that I had been carrying around for a long period of time.

So, at this point in my life, I was dealing with a divorce, dealing with physical illnesses that had manifested, and crying uncontrollably at the drop of a hat I asked myself on a daily—if not hourly—basis, "What the heck was I thinking? How can all this be productive?" I was tired of being emotional, tired of being tired, and tired of being me.

There were a few times I wished that, just like we go into a grocery store, I could walk into a life store and say, "Sorry. May I get a refund or an exchange on my life? It doesn't suit me very well. I'm happy to trade it in if that works better for you."

I would imagine God standing on the other side of the counter saying, "Sorry, there are no refunds or exchanges. You just have to make do with what you were given."

"This sucks," I would think as I walked away.

Anyone who says healing is not the most difficult thing to do has most likely never healed themselves from something. I can tell you from firsthand experience, it sucks while you're right in the middle of it.

This level of healing also occurs in the workplace: leaders who you feel don't treat you right, colleagues with whom you may have had an argument, the client who might have yelled at you. In the workplace we may not look at life through this lens. But believe me, it's healing that needs to occur.

I had to heal from being treated like a janitor when I was fully qualified to be a medical office assistant. I had to heal from giving so much of myself into an organization by working fourteen- to fifteen-hour days while feeling that the management team was not giving back. I had to heal from leaders who did not treat my strengths with respect, but rather squashed what I brought to the table. I had to heal from colleagues rejecting the process that I had just spent weeks developing. I had to heal from all the arguments and bad feelings left by fragmented relationships with coworkers. I had to heal from some of the staff terminations I have had to carry out.

Sound familiar? Not much different from our personal lives? These are just different scenarios, and yet the feelings that arise of self-forgiveness and forgiveness for others are EXACTLY the same. I believe we choose to ignore healing situations such as these because we don't want to deal with the emotions that arise, we don't have the appropriate tools to communicate how we are feeling, we don't want to bring things up that others may believe are over, and we don't want to be perceived as a negative Nelly or, worse yet, as too sensitive and emotional.

We tend to move through the workplace ignoring small grudges, pushing things under the carpet, and not having the time to deal with trivial issues. Then all of a sudden we find ourselves exploding over the smallest thing, unable to understand where all the emotion is coming from. Perhaps it is from all the things we swept under the carpet. Have you ever picked up your couch to mop underneath when you do your spring-cleaning? Have you ever seen the dust bunnies that have accumulated into one big ball under your couch? Next time you find yourself asking, "Wowsers! Where did all that emotion come from?" and you're not feeling so proud of the way you handled an otherwise miniscule situation, remember the big dust bunny under your couch, because that's probably how your grudges accumulated into one big grudge monster.

I was talking with a coaching client who was sharing with me how he felt he had ruined his relationship with others in the workplace by some of the things he had said to them and by some of the things he had done. I asked him what he thought his options were to rectify his relationships. He listed a few options. None of them were to go back to the fragmented relationships and simply say, "I screwed up and I apologize. I am working on being a better person and I hope that you understand."

When I asked him about this option, he said, "I didn't even consider that as an option." This option was not available to him because his ego mind was telling him that people would not respond in a nice way if he said that to them. He thought people would laugh at him or, worse, make fun of him and he would the laughingstock of the organization.

This came as no surprise to me, because that is how we are trained and we assume that is how others will react to our humbleness. Yet, some humility is crucial to our own healing, and most of the time the monsters in our head are much bigger than actual reality. Sometimes healing requires us to give our ego a back seat.

There is some level of pain in healing; however, suffering is optional. So let's be clear on what the difference is between pain and suffering. Pain is something we inevitably experience in some way, shape, or form; it could be physical or emotional. It is what we experience when we break up a relationship or move away from home or a loved one dies. This pain is normal. We can feel the pain of healing and sit with the emotion, whatever that emotion may be. The critical components are taking the energy of the emotion, knowing who to reach out to for support, doing something about the situation, and creating action from it.

On the other hand, I have experienced suffering as well, where I would think about the same situation again and again or replay a conversation in my head again and again but do nothing with it; it simply occupied head space with the replays. Suffering is where we actually choose to stay in suffering. We have the choice to allow it to linger and take up space in our head. The times that I would sit rehashing the same situation over and over again in my head were times of suffering. I was literally making myself suffer, which was unnecessary. The ideal situation would have been to feel the emotion of the pain fully, embrace it, and move on by doing something about it.

Once I started to do that, each time I healed the emotion better and faster. Now when something comes up, I am able to feel what I need to feel and stop before the unnecessary suffering begins.

When I first started healing some of my past wounds, I would often cry for days about the same situation. I would think about it again and again and keep circling in and out of various emotions. Experiencing it again and again was suffering.

When I was younger, my grandmother often used to say, "Jivi, you think so much that if you were whipping milk to make butter, the whole village could be fed!"

Yes, from a very young age, I would think and think and think some more. Even at work, I would create a plan and spend hours perfecting each component, and even then have contingency plans for each section, just in case. Good heavens, I think I had contingency plans for contingency plans. So, how do you heal a conditioning that is so deep that you don't know you have been conditioned to think it? This is tough, knowing you are working and acting from a place of mental conditioning.

A couple of days ago, I was given some disappointing news about a contract that I had really been looking forward to doing. I had been interviewed three times, and I absolutely loved the organization and people. Their rigorous interview process had me even more excited to work with them as an organization. Without even being consciously aware, I had set high hopes and expectations, and of course each time that happens, the Universe has a different plan. I was informed that I did not get the role, and to be honest, it felt like a punch in the gut and I cried some tears.

Ten minutes later, I was off to the races again, asking myself, "What do I need to do today that will excite me?" For weeks my marketing team had been asking me to start doing video blogs. So I thought, "What the heck! That would be fun to do." So I did my very first video blog. Within hours, we had hit over four thousand views! Moving out of the disappointment into action created a momentum of energy that was reciprocated by the Universe.

Be sure you know the difference between feeling the pain for the benefit of healing and stewing in suffering, which has no positive outcome other than maybe a headache that a pharmaceutical company may benefit from.

Sitting with all the emotions that arise when going through a healing process is probably what people fear the most. We think that the pain of going through the healing may be something we can't handle. We may be correct.

There have been times in my life when I felt like I would fall apart and I would have no one to pull me together. On one occasion I cried for a couple of days, processing all the things that had happened in boarding school in India, particularly the first time I stood in line for the morning uniform check. I had no idea what to expect. We all lined up and the warden checked our nails and made sure our shoes were polished and our uniforms ironed. As the warden walked by, I stretched out my arms to show her my nails and within a matter of a second, I was hurled down the concrete stairs, having been slapped for not having a button on my shirt. I was dumbfounded. I had not the faintest clue why I had been slapped.

I recalled that morning in India while lying on my couch in Nanaimo, crying uncontrollably. My children were with me. At some point, they called my friend and asked her to come over, as they did not know what to do with me anymore. She traveled from the mainland to be with me to support my healing journey. The Universe always knows who to send to help you in every situation.

As she stood in my kitchen and prepared some dinner for us, I lay there sobbing in deep grief. Everything seemed as though it had just happened yesterday. Sometimes we don't have to do it alone. Support is readily available should you reach out. My friend sat beside me, holding my hand, not saying a word, simply listening as I sat there crying and asking myself so many questions, questions that had no answers. I cried for hours that day, processing so many memories, and reflecting on where my life had led me.

Sometimes all you need is for someone to make you a cup of tea, touch your knee, and say, "Don't you worry. Everything will be okay."

Sometimes healing is intentional, such as when you schedule an appointment with a healer. At other times it's totally unpredictable, and you just start crying in the car going somewhere and you don't even know why. Can you make it okay to feel everything you are feeling in that moment in time, exactly where you are?

There have been many times when I have said to friends, "I feel like I am in a bit of a funk and I have no idea why." It's perfectly okay to not know the reason. Each time I think I have healed from something, it comes back full circle from a different angle.

Mountains of Healing

My greatest mountain of healing was yet to come. I knew that processing my twenty-year marriage that ended in divorce would be my greatest mountain to climb when it came to healing. Not only was I healing what went wrong in the marriage, but I was also healing the arrangement that my parents had made for me to marry this man. Everything was interconnected—my logistical marriage, my relationship with myself, my relationship with my ex-husband, my relationship with my parents, my relationship with my siblings, and yes, you guessed it, my relationship with my work boss at the time.

As I started to dissect what had happened in my marriage, I realized that my husband and I simply were incompatible and always had been. My Indian society says, "In arranged marriages, you learn to love." I had never learned to love; I had just learned to be a responsible wife and mother. I had grown spiritually and was not feeling respected for that growth.

When I think about all the things that went wrong in our marriage, I realize I was growing at an exponential rate while my partner was content staying exactly where he was. I had started to desire more out of a relationship, such as interaction and dialogue, and he was just not emotionally available in that way for me. The reverse had happened for him—he wanted me to be more financially responsible and I was not giving him what he wanted. Even though I used to say things like "I was such a great wife. He should have been happy that I stayed so long when he was the one that was at fault," I had to turn around all these thoughts and face them as well. Each person around us is a reflection of who we are, right?

I had been ready to blame everyone, so I was also healing my questions around why my parents would marry me to him. Of course, I decided it was their entire fault. Then, of course, I threw in my siblings, "who really didn't get what I was going through." Ah, how many people can one person blame for one situation? In my case, as many as I could find. I had done anything to save myself from taking responsibility for the situation I was in.

I also doubted myself and wondered how I could have done things differently.

Chapter 7

Then a day finally came when I asked myself, "What part did I play in the misery of my relationship?" My marriage was over and I could only self-forgive for any part that I had played, whether it was 1 percent or 50 percent. It's important to remember that accepting responsibility does not mean we accept all responsibility. We can only be accountable for our part. Accepting there was a role that I played was essential for my recovery. This is when the real healing begins—when we take responsibility for our part of the situation. I had hidden the pain about my marriage too well. When I got divorced, it really shocked everyone, even my parents and siblings, because I had never spoken about being miserable or unhappy.

When we don't deal with our pain, it simply remains dormant inside of us and shows up in unanticipated ways in other parts of our life. It manifests in various ways until such time as we acknowledge the pain, begin to understand its roots, and then actually do something about it. Can you imagine some of the things we carry around for decades? Do you think that is actually necessary? At some point, a burden becomes so heavy that the pain of carrying it far outweighs acknowledging it and dealing with the emotions that arise from it. Have you noticed that the greatest pain we feel is quite often connected with the ones we love and trust the most? When I think about my divorce after a twenty-year marriage, broken friendships, pain for the pain one of my children is going through, it would appear that the greatest pain comes from the ones dearest to my heart. How could it not be? Where there is love and things turn out differently from what we anticipated, there is greater pain.

Exercise—Five Crucial Steps in the Spiritual and Emotional Self-Healing Process

Remember, healing actually begins with a conscious intent to do the work. No one can do this work for you. Believe me—I tried that! Think about the stories that play the most frequently in your head and select one story that you would like to practice this exercise with. Once you have gone through the healing, your heart opens up to new levels of self-love and forgiveness. You are even better prepared to help others who are going through something similar around you.

What I have learned in my process of healing is that there are five crucial steps in the spiritual and emotional self-healing process.

1. Acknowledge and Accept

In this step, you acknowledge and accept that there is something within you that needs to be healed. You cannot heal what you don't think even exists, no matter whether it is something physical, mental, emotional, or spiritual.

2. Embrace and Understand

In this next step, embrace the story that is ready to be healed and consider who you may reach out to for help on your journey going forward. If you are uncomfortable reaching out to someone else, then meditate to gain some understanding of what the story is that you are trying to heal.

3. Dig Deep and Pull Out the Root

At first you may just get some surface answers, and you may start to feel some emotion. Don't allow this emotion to stop or hinder your healing process. Ask yourself what you think is the cause of the situation, and then ask yourself why. Continue to ask yourself why until such time as you have no more answers. This is called "root cause analysis." We are applying basic business principles to our personal journey. Be very kind and gentle with yourself during this step, as it may take days or even weeks to go through this phase.

4. Plant Forgiveness

Now, in the space that you have created by digging deep inside your soul, start to plant self-forgiveness. What will it take for you to forgive yourself? What will it take for you to forgive other people who may be involved? There have been times in my life when I simply was not ready to forgive, and that's perfectly okay as well. When we make actual choices we make them consciously, and that's all that matters at this point. Just be prepared that you may have to come back to forgiveness later.

5. Maintenance Weeding

This is a pivotal part of the healing journey, when every so often you think about a particular situation and see if any emotions arise. You continue this weeding process until you can recite the story to yourself or someone else without shedding any tears. Please remember that when you first start this healing process, it may feel impossible that you will ever get to a place of no tears. Rest assured, it always happens. You just have to be gentle, patient, and kind to yourself. Healing is a journey, and each time we move along it we move closer and closer to the destination of self-love.

Exercise—Suffering Be Gone

We can experience pain in various forms, whether relational, financial, career, or physical. The key to consider is whether we can accept the pain without festering in suffering.
1. What pain am I going through at this moment?
2. How long have I been in pain? Is the pain physical, emotional, psychological, or another type?
3. How long have I blamed, resented, or envied others because of this pain?
4. Am I fully willing to accept the pain, feel the pain, and accept every emotion attached to the pain?
5. Only when you accept every part of the pain to be a part of your journey can you stop the suffering and breathe. With each outgoing breath, slowly LET GO.

Chapter 8 Whole People

Marrying My Second Husband

I met my second husband on a trip to India in 2011. We quickly became very good friends and had a lot of fun being in each other's company. I don't think I could even name a time when I had laughed so hard as I did that particular visit to India. At that time I did not understand that my relationship with him was about love rather than friendship. It would be months later when I would recognise that we were actually in love.

This was not a typical relationship, let alone a typical marriage. There was a huge age difference between us; we were incompatible from an educational and career perspective, nor did we share any common interests. All we knew was that there was a strange relationship that we could not explain. Some might explain our relationship by saying we were soul mates or twin flames or some other name for a relationship that has no logical explanation.

It made no sense. I was willing to stake everything for this relationship, including my parents, my siblings, and anything that might be a barrier for us to be together. I was in love and nothing else mattered, or so I thought. The common thread that bound us was our thirst for traveling to spiritual and religious places around India. This one common element led to us making a decision to marry each other against all odds.

My decision to marry him came from the logic that there is no need to date anyone if you know that's who your partner will be. What I did not recognize from this place of so-called love was that there were many factors in play during this time. I was in a vulnerable state, I desired to feel loved and cared about, and I was in a panic because my ex-husband had already remarried. A panic set in that I would be left alone for the rest of my life and this gentleman was the best thing that could happen to me. I was in love.

"He is a taxi driver, Jivi. What are you thinking?" "You have lost your mind." "You have gone crazy." "He is just using you to come to Canada." "He will cheat on you because all he cares about is coming to Canada." People made comment after comment about how we were destined to fail at this marriage. I can honestly look back today and say that those few months when I felt I was in love were some of the best times of my life, filled with laughter, fun, and light-heartedness. We spent much of our time for almost two years in a long-distance relationship, with me traveling back and forth to India.

Even immigration made it next to impossible for him to come to Canada. We had one of the most difficult Canadian immigration cases possible, as we did not fit the immigration criteria. Not only was he younger than I was, he also had less education and did not have the same caliber of job as I did, according to Citizenship and Immigration Canada. To top it off, my parents did not consent to the marriage; in order to immigrate to Canada, Indians have to be married with their parents' consent. We were facing some major immigration problems.

I had gone to India as the authorities had asked so that they could interview both of us and make a decision about whether or not they would give my husband a Canadian visa to move to Canada. We had a genuine case, we had followed all the immigration rules, and we were fully prepared to answer all the questions they might have for us. We had talked through all the things that could possibly go wrong. We had perfect mitigation plans and contingencies for each mitigation.

So, to cut a long story short, we had the interview and after four exhausting hours of answering some extremely personal questions, the authorities told us that they would let us know their decision in two weeks. Less than two weeks later, we received a letter in the mail informing us that they had decided we were not in a genuine marriage and that they would not allow my husband to immigrate to Canada. My life, and my husband's and my future, rested in the hands of someone who had interviewed us for four hours and, based on culture and traditions, he had decided that we did not have the right to be together.

That is where the real challenge began when implementing what I thought was my personal journey. After much crying and shedding lots of tears, I started to go through the options. Having my sponsorship for him to come to Canada turned down was not an issue we had even considered, as we thought there was no way they could refuse an immigration visa to someone who had been visited by his wife in India thirteen times in two years to be with her husband, right? Wrong. Yes, they could, and yes, they did.

It felt similar to what happens in a workplace in which you have a clear strategy and know exactly what you want to do and how to do it. Then a situation happens that totally throws you off your game. It's like dodging balls and adjusting your game with a new strategy all the time.

You must be wondering what happened with Citizenship and Immigration Canada afterwards and whether my husband ever made it to Canada. Yes, he did, but with a new strategy, of course. I had to appeal his case in the Supreme Court of

Canada by myself to prove that we loved each other. Yes, you that read correctly: to prove that we loved each other.

Can you imagine a court case having to prove love?

There we were, back at the drawing board, trying to figure out how we could provide evidence of our love. So, we collected thousands of pictures of us together, intimate, goofy, and casual ones. There were about two thousand in total. We collected every receipt for gifts we had purchased for each other. We gathered receipts for all the traveling we had done together.

You may think that was enough, but no. The saga continued. At the court hearing, I was once again asked a series of personal questions and drilled about the details of our relationship. During the hearing, I asked the judge if I could share a story that might put everything to rest one way or the other and he said yes.

I told him that during each visit to India, it was common for me to get very ill, usually with diarrhea and vomiting. On one such visit, I had become so ill that I was not able to make it to the bathroom in time and I soiled all my clothes and the bedsheets. I woke up my husband and was crying uncontrollably, shaking with embarrassment. He quickly sat up, wiped my tears, and asked me not to worry about a thing. He carried me to the bathroom where he ran the hot water and helped me take a shower to get cleaned up. Inside my heart, I was so worried about the dirty sheets. What would his parents think when they woke up the morning? I wasn't a child; I was a grown woman, for heaven's sake. How could I not have made it to the bathroom?

As I rested my face on his chest for a moment to catch my breath, he said, "Why don't you put on these clean clothes and I will be back in just a moment."

I slowly started to get dressed in the clothes he had hung

out for me in the bathroom, and with an embarrassed heart I walked reluctantly back into the bedroom. I anticipated my next move would be to wash the sheets before anyone woke up. I walked into the room and to my surprise my husband had taken all the sheets and was washing them by hand and hanging them to dry. And he had put clean sheets on the bed.

That night, I just crawled back into bed and went to sleep. The next morning, he had already folded the sheets and put them away inside the cupboard before the family even woke up. I looked over at him and started to cry. He knew how I would feel and made sure that everything was clean.

This may not be a big deal to many of you, but to me, this is what captured my heart—that someone was not only willing to clean up after me but also felt my heart's anguish and did what was necessary to take that anguish away.

At this point, I turned to the judge and said, "If that was not love, I don't know what else would show you that he loves me and I love him."

I surrendered to the decision that the judge would make, and he granted permission for my husband to get a permanent residence visa and be allowed into Canada.

My second husband arrived in Canada at the end of 2014. I had made such a pretty picture, imagining in my head how we would live together. Everything would be just fine—we loved each other and that was all that mattered. Little did we know that living together with the reality and practicality of sharing this household would be so different from loving each other during a period of vacation.

Soon after he arrived, we started to have conflicts about where to live, how to pay the expenses, about having children, and where his parents would live. We did not discuss all these very practical aspects of our life upfront because we were in love and we thought that was all that mattered. We had made a huge assumption that all we needed was love and everything else would simply resolve itself.

To this day, we are still trying to work it out. We have nothing but love and caring for each other, and we have learned we do not have to be miserable in a relationship. Where this relationship will go, I still don't know. But I do know two things for sure. One, we both love each other and care a great deal about each other, and two, it's okay to not know and to take things day by day for now. I continue to learn many things from this patch of the costume. Among other things, with their life experiences, your parents do know best. I learned what love feels like; I also learned what the pain of love feels like. The greatest lesson of all for me is that love IS NOT enough; there must be a realistic practicality to our relationships as well.

Showing Up at Work as a Whole Person

This whole saga was going on at the very same time that I was working full time and showing up to work under these circumstances of stress and overwhelm. To say that I was on edge was an understatement. I had a low tolerance of what people were asking of me, I had low patience with what I considered incompetence, and my listening skills were poor. I found myself asking lots of questions after a meeting because my mind had wandered into how I needed to prepare my case for the courts. It was impossible to segregate the Jivi who was dealing with immigration at home from the person who showed up at work. All I could do was pretend well and try to keep my head in the game as much as possible. But inside my head was a tornado of thoughts.

Knowing what was going on for me, just take a moment

to imagine me sitting at a meeting around a boardroom table, smiling and pretending to be fully present. How many times have you yourself done that? You are in a meeting, your thoughts carry you away, and before you know it, time has passed and you have no idea what the conversation is about anymore. Be truthful with yourself: How much time do you think you spend on personal issues when you are actually on a paycheck? The employer pays for us to be fully present in our job. That includes occupying our mind with efficiency ideas, quality improvement ideas, new services, and product brainstorming. If you can relate to how much time you spend thinking about personal issues at work, multiply that time by how many team members you have. This knowledge doesn't mean you have to do something about it, but at least be real with yourself about how much time is consumed by frivolous and irrelevant thoughts at work on someone else's time clock.

Becoming a Strategic Leader

When I became a strategic leader, I made a point of touching base with each person on the team at least once a quarter to see how things were going in their life. I would particularly ask about their stress levels and how they were managing them. At these meetings, we would chat, laugh, and talk about life, not about work. It was my way of getting to know them as human beings first and employees second. We called these "just-because meetings," in which there was no agenda; we simply got on the phone and started with "Hello, how have you been?" Then I would listen until such time as their heart was empty and mine was full. I would send my team members birthday wishes and personalize each message based on what they had been through that year, and I sent them a prayer for the coming year.

I can almost hear you thinking, "Do you know how much time that would take?" And yes, I do know how much time it takes, because I did it. When you ask past employees under my leadership, they will tell you that my legacy is not all the strategy work that I did but the birthday messages and our just-because calls, because those made them feel like they mattered as whole people. Nurturing starts at the leadership level. If people see you treating your self-care with importance, they will follow suit. If they see you reflecting stress, anxiety, and constant overwhelm, they will make the assumption that that is what success looks like to you and, being master mimickers, they will copy your behavior.

Showing Up at Work in the Middle of Our Storm

We each show up at work with some sort of storm going on at any given time—we might have had an argument with our spouse; maybe we are dealing with our child skipping school; we might have been diagnosed with some sort of illness; there might be financial surprises we did not expect; we might have recently become a caregiver to others. We could be dealing with an unlimited number of things at any given time, and we still have to show up at work. It is impossible to leave these small or big storms that we call "life" at home. They impact us in the workplace through our communications, through how we handle conflict, how we help each other, how much we are willing to give back, and how creative we feel. Like it or not, we get a paycheck to be at work, and that includes having your mind at work. Yet, if you are realistic, how much time do you spend thinking about your own storms while you are on the job?

Embracing these storms so that we are present in each

moment in the workplace means being hypervigilant of our surroundings. It means giving each other the time that is needed to listen, and it means being yourself regardless of the situation. In a perfect-world organization, we would also be in that place where we simply do things for others without any expectations in return.

I have worked as part of a team where that was possible. After six years, our project was nearing its conclusion. I will never forget our last team event. I found myself saying something that I would have never anticipated. I talked about corporate love and how this organization had taught me that it is possible to have love in the workplace. For the first time in my life, I was able to get up on stage and say how proud I was to be a part of an organization where I truly felt loved and had the freedom to show that I cared about each individual person on the team.

Can you imagine for a moment working in an environment in which people genuinely care about each other and show compassion openly; an environment in which you develop strong relationships where people trust each other's intentions; an environment in which a friend is there for you regardless of what is going on for them?

In one of my most recent workplaces, we nurtured each and every person and paid close attention to what was going on in their personal lives and the issues that might impact the work they were doing. More often than not, my conversations with our team members were more along the lines of how they were doing in their lives, what their aspirations were, how their personal life was impacting the work, and what they thought I could do to support their dreams and goals.

When it came time to do performance reviews, we did self-reviews, in which the team member reviewed how they thought they had performed over the year. This review included questions such as "Over the last year, what are you the most proud of? What are some things you want to improve upon, personally and professionally? And above all, what do you want to do over the coming year as a personal goal for yourself?" This methodology allows the individual to be in the driver's seat to share what they think about their performance rather than having the leader be in charge.

There are some absolute downsides as well to approaching work in this way, as sometimes there can be fine lines between what you should know and what you should not know. I believe this is why leadership is changing; some leaders are ill-equipped to handle the whole person showing up at work. When people show up to work with all their baggage, it seems much easier to say, "Leave your problems at home." If leaving problems at home is impossible, the problems will manifest as sick days, stress leaves, a rise in workplace conflict, and even grievances.

As I sit here reminiscing about the downsides of the bring-your-whole-self-to-work concept, five things stand out for me that I originally considered as downsides. I was later surprised by what else I learned. I will also share what I learned about these downsides to ease your mind.

Downsides to Learning about Your Employees as Whole People

1. Time Consumption

You may be thinking that connecting with each individual person is a huge time commitment and, given today's fast-paced world, next to impossible. You are absolutely correct in thinking it requires time to connect with people at a deep level. However, the benefits of return on long-term investment are also true, such as higher levels of dedication to the work, increased loyalty to the leadership's vision, and higher retention rates; we all know how time-consuming it is to hire, orient, and train new team members.

2. Skills Inventory

A perception of another downside may be the level of skill the leader may have in the areas of coaching, communication, facilitation, and conflict resolution. There are few ways to rectify this. The leader must either gain these basic skills, as he will need them in all walks of life, or hire someone who provides coaching support and whose role it is to simply stay connected.

I can't even count how many times some random check-in call with a team member yielded an efficiency gain, a quality improvement idea, or brainstorming around a new project. These random check-ins are amazing, as I was able to connect directly with the people doing the work; these are the people who know best how efficiency can be gained.

3. Not My Job

Many of you may be thinking it is really not my job to be "babysitting" people and checking in to see how their personal lives are doing. To this, I ask but one simple question: How is what you're doing now working out for you? Let's be honest here. If it were working out for you, you would not be reading this book.

Our job today requires a level of creativity that may not have been required in the past, and we can only be creative if we have a clear and calm mind.

4. Knowing Too Much

One of the other greatest worries I hear is, "What if they tell me something that I should not know?" I have worked with multiple teams over a thirty-year span, and yet I have only had two cases that I truly did not know what to do with. They might have disclosed too much in the beginning; however, the situation ended with them getting the appropriate support they needed.

Sometimes, we have to put our leadership aside and just be a human being first. Think for a moment whom you consider to be your leadership idol. Most likely that person had great skills in the areas of relationship building, listening, humbleness, and assertiveness, and when you spoke to them, you felt heard, acknowledged, and appreciated. So, I would ask you, if your odds were as low as mine over a thirty-year period, do you not want to take the chance to impact the hundreds of people who will not disclose to the level that you are afraid of?

5. They Are Paid, So They Should Just Do Their Job

No doubt they "should just do their job." However, what I found in the last six years of my career was that when I spent time with each person and made them feel like they mattered, they did meaningful and purposeful work with passion. That's a very different approach from "just doing their job."

Life happens to each of us, and some of us have become masters at living two lives, one at home and one at work. I believe living two lives comes from more of a fear base, such as "I don't really have the skills required to handle the person in front of me." This would include fear that the person might share they may have an alcohol problem or they are going through a divorce or they have a child whom they worry about.

If we believe that people around us reflect back to us what we need to see, then what does this statement say about how happy and content we are with the work that we do?

I can truly, genuinely say that in the last six years of my career, I was very involved in the personal matters of each member of our team—as much as they wanted to share, of course—and I have to say, that was the happiest work environment I have ever been in.

∾

Don't get me wrong; we were a fast-paced work environment and we had a lot to prove in a very short time. We had a leader who had a clear strategy, from the vision to the goals and from the milestones to the key success factors. As a team, we knew exactly what we were doing and how to do it, and yet we had some moving pieces each day. The beauty resided in our having the freedom to nurture each team member through a variety of things such as Mindfulness Training each Friday as an optional virtual call, "Golden Nugget" training days (soft skills training in communication, conflict, and facilitation), and (the best day) Virtual Watercooler meetings on Monday mornings. These were literally just like a watercooler conversation—we talked about anything. I remember one call, we talked about the significance of turbans in Sikhism. Some might perceive these meetings as time wasters, and yet we as a team were getting results like no other program, well exceeding our goals each time by 30 to 40 percent.

One day, I was training an existing team member in one of

the new facilitation techniques, because we were moving from a "tell them what to do" approach to a more organic approach of "let's ask them what they want to do." My team member had already started the meeting when I arrived, and I quietly sat in the back, waiting for her to finish her sentence. She normally would ask a lot of questions of the group and get feedback, but that day I noticed she was not asking questions; rather, she was simply giving them information as though she had pre-recorded the conversation in her head.

When there was a bit of a break, I introduced myself to the gathering and asked for a ten-minute break to catch up with my team member. As we walked outside, I asked her, "Did you notice anything about what was going on around you?"

She responded, "No, I was telling them all about the benefits of the program and they seemed to be listening eagerly."

I told her that one person was typing while she was speaking, another was washing some dishes in the background, another was looking at his shoes, and the last one had a glazed look on her face, most likely with no clue as to what was being said. We had only a few minutes before going back into the room, so we had to make a plan very quickly about how to move forward. She asked me to lead the next part while she observed what I was talking about.

We walked into the room together and I said, "You all seemed a bit distracted previously, so I am concerned that we may be missing the mark of making this meeting valuable to you."

To the surprise of both of us, one person spoke up and said, "We are not sure why you are meeting with us, because the decision-maker is not even in the room. We just work here."

I asked what it would take to get the decision-maker in the room, and we were informed a simple phone call would have him with us in fifteen minutes.

Sigh.

So, let's dissect this situation for a minute and gain some insight into the team member who had shown up to facilitate that meeting. She had been contemplating retirement for herself over the last few weeks while we were implementing a new technique as to how to approach our work. Do you think she would have a vested interest in learning and delivering a new technique? Her personal and professional choices were conflicting and impacting how she was showing up at work. And she was totally oblivious.

Let's flip this scenario to look at it from another angle. If someone had asked her whether learning a new technique while she was contemplating retirement was exciting to her, she might have been honest and we would not have found ourselves in that situation. We would have saved ourselves the first four hours into this meeting, as she would have identified the disconnection between herself and everyone else, asked the right questions, and learned we needed the decision-maker in the room.

Over the past six years, story after story has indicated that we can't separate the problems of the person from the person who shows up to work. A person will show up to work as they are, and we only see glimpses of their stories peeking through, like symptoms we may not fully understand. When someone shows up to work feeling paralyzed by some life choice they need to make, they are very easy to spot if you are aware of what the baseline is for that team member's personality. You will only know this baseline if you have spent time getting to know them. They may appear distracted when you're speaking to them, or you may perceive them as not listening in a meeting, underperforming at something they are very skilled at, or simply on edge and reacting to things that normally would not bother them.

The Three-Attribute Game

I remember playing a game with our team one day. We were sitting around ten tables. I asked each person to write down three attributes that they felt were the top strengths for each person at the table. We rotated people through each table so that each person had the opportunity to add attributes to their coworkers' names that were not there already. Each person was also to put their own top three attributes on an index card to compare it with what people had written about them. There was not one single person who had more than one or two attributes the same as the ones other people had written about them.

I will share my own story around what was said about me. People listed my three attributes as "persuasion," "compassion," and "listening." For myself, I had "listening," "empathy," and "collaboration." I was in shock with the word "persuasion"; to me it felt synonymous with "manipulation." I was surprised that people would perceive me that way. It took a couple of weeks for me to process this word, and then finally I asked my coworker if he thought I was persuasive. He responded, "Absolutely. When you believe in something, you can get anyone to follow you to the ends of the earth, because you lead from the heart, with passion."

So, "persuasion" was actually a good thing. Intriguing.

But do you see how my definition of "persuasion" was so different from the definition of those around me? I would never have identified myself with that characteristic at all. Sometimes, it takes an outsider to show us how we are being perceived by others.

As a leader, don't shy away from having these conversations with people and doing team activities that help them see how others perceive them.

Holding up the mirror and really looking inside yourself requires courage, more courage than anything else you can do. Do you have the strength, courage, and stamina to take a hard look at how you are behaving and being perceived?

"Jivi, You Don't Listen"

Just recently I was visiting one of my spiritual mentors and she said something intriguing to me. She said, "Jivi, you don't listen."

I have to be honest—I was shocked and surprised by this statement. People around me have always told me that listening is my greatest skill, and I take much pride in listening extremely well. This was going to be a hard pill to swallow; I needed some processing time on this one.

As usual, she said to me, "Why don't you sleep on it?" When she said that, I knew I probably wouldn't sleep at all! As I laid my head down on the pillow, I realized how fortunate I was to be lying there on an actual pillow. I thought, "How many people are there in the world who don't have a pillow tonight?"

As I expressed my gratitude and sent love everywhere in the world, the sentence kept replaying in my head: "Jivi, you don't listen." I started to think back to pivotal moments in my life, and I could name situation after situation in which I did not listen to anyone because I am so headstrong that if I want to do something, I do it at all costs.

"Jivi," I thought, "no, you don't listen!" Wow, how was it that my mentor could pose a statement, let me "sleep on it," and get me to this place? So, in the morning, I woke up to a wonderful cup of cardamom tea. As I sat beside her, I said, "Okay, maybe I don't listen."

Her response was phenomenal and one I wish I had

recorded. She said, "Okay. Now that we have that out of the way, let's move on."

"Wait, wait," I thought. "I need to know why you said what you did!"

Without hearing my question, she responded, "Jivi, you need to know how headstrong you are when you want to do something. This requires you to be focused and clear. Not listening is not necessarily a bad thing. It means you are able to do whatever you set your mind to. It also means that going forward you need to consider what other people are advising you to do as well, especially in areas where you don't have expertise."

How this ties in to the blaming others will be fascinating indeed for you. In each one of these scenarios I blamed someone else for the results, and yet I was the one who did not listen to those exact people. When you consider my work story above and this more recent learning, they had one thing in common: I was not listening to my physical, emotional, spiritual, or mental bodies.

Exercise—Factors for Creating a Safe Environment at Work

So, let's see what factors are vital to creating a safe environment at work, so that there is little to no fear and therefore less and less of the blame game is played. Here are some tips in creating and fostering a mindful culture.
- Define your values as an organization, and when recruiting keep those values at the core of each conversation. Ask questions of people to describe

situations in their life that may be significant to those particular values. Then in orientation give examples of how you walk the talk of your organizational values. Orientation is the first and most beneficial place at which to foster what you want exemplified. Our core values at my most recent workplace were authenticity and humbleness, and we fostered these by having authentic conversations at the leadership level and not having credentials on our business cards. If you cannot connect to another human being at a basic human level, the credentials are simply alphabet soup behind a name.

- In meetings or in a company newsletter, ask people to share stories about how their values have been tested in the field and what they did to overcome the challenge. This ensures that the entire organization knows you are serious about upholding those values at all levels of the organization.
- Foster an organizational language around respect, authenticity, and transparency, in which people have an in-depth understanding of what those values mean to them personally and to the organization. At some point, people should be using common definitions.
- Foster an environment in which each person feels safe to say what's on their mind, by ensuring you have meetings at which it is clear that there will be no reprimands or consequences to the conversation. People are very smart and can pick up quickly if your intentions are not genuine, so be careful you have your intentions in check, with no judgment and with the intention of simply listening.

> - Build a trusting environment by exemplifying that you hold people's personal information in confidence and don't use it for manipulative purposes. Each piece of information people share with you builds a shared understanding of respect and confidence in your leadership.
> - There are a few things that have no place in a healthy organization. Toxicity, gossip, rumor, and disrespect. Each of these should be dealt with immediately to send the right message to everyone that these things will not be tolerated. In the orientation, I would tell new recruits that the leadership team bends over backward to support our staff but we have zero tolerance for toxicity and gossip. I would coach people to have the right conversation with the right person whenever they felt a concern. When someone complains to you as a leader, it's as simple as saying, "May I know what is important to you about telling me this story?" This gives them the indication that you know there may be some underlying motivation and you want that to be on the table. I have also said, "What can I do to support your conversation with the right person?"

You can spot someone who is playing the blame game very easily: for instance, if somebody makes you feel drained when you converse with them, because nothing seems to be going right for them. They complain about how little money they make, how their spouse treats them, how management doesn't know what they're doing, how the restaurant they went to last night had horrible food, how they hurt themselves doing something fun, and how they had a bad time at the movies. These statements are not one-off statements, because, let's be real, these things happen to all of us at one time or another. The repetitive nature of this person's complaints helps us know they have the "why me?" complex.

No doubt you can think of someone who does this. And I ask you, could you be that person to someone else? What if you do identify with that person and know this is totally you? I know you would never say it to anyone else; your secret is safe with me. However, do something about it—take action, stop being a pawn in your own game. It's probably not fun anyway. It's pretty draining when you have to uphold a level of the pseudo-self most of the time. Not to mention you will find yourself, like me a few years back, with no one left to blame. Then it's even tougher, because you start to blame yourself.

If you find that you are dealing with a blaming and complaining person in the work environment, find a way to let them know they are impacting people with their style of communication. For example, I may say something like, "Have you considered how other team members may perceive you?" If they are oblivious of how others perceive them, share with them how you feel being around them and ask them how you, as a leader, can support them in giving a different perception going forward.

I remember asking an employee once, "Do you truly mean to come across as rude as you sound, or is that just the perception you want to create?" What that question tells the team member is that their behavior is not going unnoticed. If that is not the perception they want to create, help them define how they want to be perceived and make an action with that person to help them change.

Chapter 9   Tired of Wearing a Costume for Society

Imagine for a moment wearing a costume that looks like a patchwork quilt sewn together with buttons. Each patch is individually and delicately interwoven with detail, color, and stitching. You eagerly adorn this beautiful patchwork costume, because you have made each patch carefully and precisely, and sewn it together over many years. You have played close attention to each and every detail, sometimes even restitching the patch several times.

Now realize that each patch piece in this costume represents one or even several of the stories you tell yourself about your life, and what others have said about you or to you. Consider the amount of detail you recall about a particular life experience and the amount of time you have thought about the story, over and over again. "I could have done this differently. I should have said this. If only they had done this, I would have been that."

We rehash the story several times, and at some point we conclude our personal truth about the story and that patch gets beautifully added to our costume of experiences. We take pride in these patches, because we have thought about them so much and have spent so much time in the intricate details of "I should have, I could have, and I would have" in the story.

Think of each button on the costume reflecting everything we failed at. Imagine the zipper on this costume as we continue to become these stories. We even love the shoes that go with this costume, the shoes being all our life experiences, the ones we carry around, thinking we cannot let them go. Each and every patch serves its own purpose in covering us up from the world. We take each experience seriously because we want to take pride in the patchwork of our costume. We have come to believe that the story we are telling ourselves in that exact way is the truth, and we reinforce it again and again by remembering the same story again and again in the same way. At some point in our life, this costume becomes heavy and all the patchwork that we had taken such pride in becomes unbearable and unwearable.

My Costume Became Unbearable

In 2010, my costume had become unbearable. It had become too heavy and I was tired of carrying it around and wanted to be free of it. My broken marriage, my unhappy career, all the various roles I was playing, all my life experiences, even my education, all contributed to my costume of being "somebody." This somebody had no identity of her own but rather had only a beautiful costume sewn together by what everyone else wanted her to be. Supposedly, this costume was what society wanted to believe adorns an accomplished person who has a great job, a great life, lots of money, the perfect body, and their entire life made for them.

Each experience you have read about so far in this book was perfectly aligned as a patch on my costume. My life experiences became my costume. My perceived failures became my buttons. My view of success became my shoes. The thread that sewed it all together came from other people validating my costume, other people being my friends and family, who unintentionally said things like, "Wow! Being away from your parents must have been hard when you were in boarding school. How did you survive being away from home? Why would your parents send you away like that?"

Of course, there were many more comments and questions from people who could not comprehend the decisions my parents had made for me. Each comment from people beautifully reinforced my costume, so that it would become stronger and stronger and harder and harder to remove.

Having gone through the healing for each individual patch, I know exactly when I first started to put on this costume. As I said before, it was in 1978, when I headed to India to attend boarding school. Even though I don't recall very much about the day that I left Canada for India, I do remember as clearly as if it had happened yesterday that my father and I sat on the edge of the bed in his bedroom and he said to me, "You are going to India because we want you to be 'somebody.' We want to be proud of who you become in your life."

I became an overachiever. I was determined to be "somebody." When I came back to Canada, holding one job was never enough. Over a twenty-year period, I worked two or three jobs most of the time, going from one workplace to another, sometimes working twelve- to fourteen-hour days. It was not enough to work in just one place; I needed to be "somebody." I needed to have the perfect marriage and I wanted to be the best daughter-in-law and sister-in-law, someone who upheld traditions and culture in her family.

In Grade 12 when my father asked me whether I wanted to go to university or get married and I chose marriage, I tried hard to make it work. After I was married, I pursued further education for many years, again because I needed to be "somebody." Well, that somebody fell apart and it was not pretty.

My entire world crashed down around me, and the perfect somebody was now an outcast, someone who had betrayed her family and "lost her mind."

I don't think we even realize when we put on a costume, because it is so slowly sewn together that before we know it, we are actually already sewn well into the costume of the stories. Each story has its own little patch, its own little button, with careful stitching so that it doesn't fall apart.

One day I woke up with emptiness in my heart and such a heaviness at what everyone wanted me to be, which I could no longer explain. According to everyone else, I was a "somebody," and yet I felt like a "nobody."

I started to feel the weight of the costume, doing things out of obligation, doing things just because I couldn't say no, saying things that my heart really didn't want to say, feeling guilt, resentment, and anger, and yet holding them inside. "It will get better," I would think, "next week, next month, next year, when the kids are older, things will be better." Guess what? They never did get better, no matter how hard I tried to fool myself into believing the reasons and justifications. Things never got better.

As a matter of fact, the costume just got heavier and heavier, with impacts on my physical, emotional, and spiritual body. This costume of being "somebody" for everybody else had become very heavy, and I was feeling the weight of the world patched into the seams of this costume. Nothing I did was ever good enough; nothing I said was good enough. It didn't matter how hard I tried, it simply was never good enough. There was always a lineup of people who were disappointed by something I did or said, intentionally or unintentionally. There was always someone I had left out, or something I had forgotten, or a decision I had made incorrectly.

It's actually quite funny, really, when you think about

it—this costume we wear comes from our perception of success and our expectation of the roles that we should be playing in our relationships. Most of the time, we build an illusion of how we should behave: what a mother should be like, how to act as a daughter, what to do to be successful at our job, what role we should be playing as a wife. Then if we don't fulfill the roles just as society teaches us, we feel guilt, resentment, and disappointment in ourselves because we are not this way or that way. It's a vicious circle of what we think we should be, comparing the reality with the feelings that arise from not being a certain way.

Quite often, we start to believe our roles in life define who we are. We look at other mothers and think, "I am not doing that, so I am a bad mom." We look at another career woman and think, "I am nowhere near where she is, so I am not successful." We look at other offspring and think, "I don't take care of my parents in that way, so I am not a very good child." There is no end to "I am not good enough."

Many of the girls in my daughter's elementary school classes had stay-at-home moms who would often bake beautiful goodies for the entire class. I would always feel guilty being a working mom. One day I went to pick her up at school, and one of the other moms told me a story. She said her daughter was given an essay to write on what her parents did at home, and she had written that her father takes his briefcase and goes to work and Mom watches her soap operas. Both of us had a good laugh about her guilt for not working and her daughter thinking she watched television all day, and my guilt for working and buying cookies from the store instead of baking them.

We have ideals in our heads and we make ourselves believe that if we fall into that structure, only then are we successful or talented or gifted in some way.

"How Are You?"

As I went through the discovery process of "Who am I?", my yoga teacher asked me how things were going. This has always been a loaded question for me. I sometimes don't know how to respond. "Should I tell her the truth about the turmoil that is going on in my heart, or do I simply say 'I am okay' or 'I am well' and just move on from the question?"

How often do you find yourself giving a robotic answer to the question "How are you?" What do you do—spill the beans of exactly what is going on in your life, or do you give a conservative answer just so you don't have to disclose a bunch of details that you feel are unnecessary?

My response to my yoga teacher that particular day was "Okay. I'm feeling a bit sad because I have to sell my house."

I had come to a financial situation that meant I would not be able to pay the mortgage of my home, so I was considering selling it to pay off all the debt I was in and moving to a smaller place. Yoga is not just about poses, as I came to know; it's about the whole person and every little thing happening in your life that impacts your physical wellbeing. I had no context as to why I was feeling sad, because like everyone else, I had no time to process and reflect.

As I sat there crying about how if I sold the home I didn't know where I was going to go, what I was going to tell the kids, and where I would move, she listened quietly. She then asked, "What does the house mean to you? What does it reflect for you?"

"What does the house mean to me?" What kind of question was that? There I was, pouring out my heart, and that's what she wanted to know.

I decided this would be the last time I was going to answer

the question "How are you?" with any level of detail. It was a good thing that I fully trusted her intention. I started to process my situation aloud. I said things like, "It's the first large purchase I have ever made on my own. I have spent so much time decorating it exactly as I want it. It means that I have safety and security, not just for me but for my kids. My kids needed a place to live."

I had a strong attachment to having purchased this home that really set the stage for doing things on my own. I had never purchased anything on my own before; either my father or my husband had helped in those decisions. Getting a mortgage, purchasing a home, and decorating it were significant factors in my freedom and liberation. I had dreamed for years about decorating my home a certain way—for me that was larger than life itself.

With my ex-husband, I had lived in a house we had intended to sell, so I had never put much up on the walls. It never did feel like a home, but rather just a house that provided a roof over our heads. A home feels different. I wanted something that depicts my colorful personality and yet feels welcoming to each person who enters the home. I wanted my home to be a safe haven and a place I could feel proud of.

But had I started to associate my success with this home? Had this home become another patch in my costume? Selling this home would mean that I had failed in some way, even though I didn't even speak to my family. I had this perception that selling my home was a failure of some kind and I wouldn't be a somebody if I sold it. When I got divorced I vowed to myself to make things work financially and show everyone that I was right in following my heart. Selling this home would mean I didn't make it financially.

How engrained we are with the stitching on our costumes.

Some things go so deeply that we are oblivious until someone asks us a question about our costume and we turn around and look in the mirror and there is the patch in clear sight, nicely decorated and well stitched. Some things work out for the best simply by talking about them. They move us into conscious awareness and then we can actually do something about them.

I was fortunate enough to have a sister who pulled me through this financial rut so I could keep my home, which continues to be a part of what I have accomplished. However, I now have a lower level of attachment to it. I am not my home, nor does it define whether I am a good person or not. This was not an easy lesson, but critical in helping me to take off the costume itself.

Wearing a Quilted Costume at Work

Think about your work environment and all your colleagues; maybe think of the last team meeting you had. Could you imagine every person in that room—including yourself—wearing a quilted costume of their own patches of life experiences? Do you think it is possible to show up at work as our true, raw, authentic personality without this costume that we wear? Not just your colleagues. Consider the people you serve as clients and other stakeholders. Each person has her stories that she carries around with her. Have you encountered a situation where you say something to someone and their reaction to you is totally out of proportion to what you just said? Have you yourself been in a situation where you have later regretted overreacting to something that normally would not even bother you?

Imagine for a minute a group of people who don't know each other coming together for a common purpose in a workplace, with each one carrying his own costume. They have come together to implement a certain strategy or project, to simply earn a paycheck, or maybe to dedicate time to our cause. The outward reason for being there may be different from the internal one, and yet we come together as a team with a common vision. There is no "I" in "team." We have been taught it is impossible to work as a team when the impact of one individual surpasses the team. Also, there is no team without nurturing each "I" who is present, at least not anymore. The days are gone when we could leave our problems at home. We have always carried our costume to work. We just were better at hiding it before. Now the symptoms are showing up as stress leaves, sick days, and increased conflict in the workplace.

I was still working full-time when I started to remove my costume of "somebody," and I know exactly how I was showing up to work before and after its removal. Don't get me wrong, removing this costume is not easy and takes time. It's one patch at a time that you work with to understand better the weaving and colors in that particular patch. You must be willing to feel raw, vulnerable, and exposed, because that is how I felt. I knew I was safe, but I still had to feel the rawness of my emotions and my vulnerability.

I asked myself, "If I am not wearing this costume, then who am I? Will people like me if I expose who I truly am?"

The first step in removing this costume in the workplace was to make sure that I was more authentic in my communication with my leadership team and my regional team. I had to really focus on effective ways to communicate my truth, rather than saying things that were not how I felt inside.

The physical space of my office started to change too. I added a lot more color because I love color. I added all kinds of little toys, and very often when I was trying to think through a problem and process some creative solutions, I would throw a sticking hand at the window. Even though people would make fun of my colorful, fun office of toys, guess where most people gathered all day? You are right if you guessed my office.

I would practice silence more often in meetings by asking myself, "If I don't say anything right now, what will we lose?" This was a different type of silence from the silence my MBA professor identified. This was a more intentional sitting back and not saying something to see what the results would be and allowing the other person to conclude something I already knew.

Silence is an amazing tool that is often overlooked. I did this because I didn't want to say something simply to fill the air because silence can be awkward.

Each day I would test how my colleagues responded to me if and when I opened up and shared my fears and vulnerabilities with them. Could I truly work moment to moment, just as I was practicing through mindfulness in my personal life? I started to look at the perceived complex problems through a lens of simplicity and came up with simple solutions. When I shared them with the team, we would often ask whether it could really be that simple, and most of the time it was. I got more comfortable asking questions and being open to communicating when I was not understanding something. I started to feel lighter and lighter at work. I was no longer trying to be someone that I am not. I stopped wearing a business suit and carrying a laptop everywhere unless it was essential. I went back to basic human-to-human interaction. Credentials are simply alphabet soup behind a name if you are not able to connect with another person from a fundamental interpersonal perspective.

I was at the peak of my leadership career, with respect from others, and yet I was authentically myself, with no costume. "How can this be possible?" I would ask myself. I thought I was nobody without my costume, but here I was, actually now a somebody, but the somebody I wanted to be, not the one society wanted me to be. The contrast was significant enough for people to take notice. I was happier, I could handle most days with grace and ease, and on the days when I was troubled, I was not afraid to speak up and ask for help.

I remember a few days over the six-year period when I called my leader and would say, "I need to vent, so I just need a listening ear, no solutions." He would be gracefully present as I continued to vent. At the end, I would say something like, "Okay. I am done. I will figure out some solutions and get back to you." I had accepted the fact that I am an empath, a high feeler, and I just need to vent some things.

As I removed this costume in my personal life, my workplace relationships were getting better. I had no grudges and was dealing with conflict much more easily. My leadership had never been better and the team was responding to me by outperforming their targets each time we checked, coupled with a high degree of trust, respect, and admiration for the leadership team.

Being Officially Disowned

Around the same time as I was slowly removing the patches, a new situation arose that I would securely sew into this costume once again. I had received a letter from my parents, and I was traveling back to Vancouver Island on a two-hour ferry ride. They had left it with my sister for her to give to me. My father had signed his name on the back over the envelope flap to discourage anyone else from opening it.

I slowly opened the letter to read what was inside. To my utter shock, it was a letter of disownment, indicating the reasons why I was being disowned and what kinds of things

I would not be allowed to do, such as not being able to attend my father's funeral. My attention quickly went to the end of the letter, which was signed and dated. I sat there staring at the signature. It felt as though my relationship had become a contract that was being terminated. It's a strange feeling, being disowned from your parents. All of a sudden you don't feel you belong anywhere and have no identity in the world.

With tears rolling down my face, I continued to read all the stipulations. To be honest, I really did not know what to make of the situation. I just remember reading it over and over again and staring at my father's signature. The letter was a copy, so he must have retained the original, for what purpose I am unsure to this day.

It seemed that, to him, I was a contract he was resigning from. They did not support my second marriage, and for that reason, they disowned me.

I thought to myself, "Is that even possible? Can you resign from being related to me? Can parents disown a child? Can they actually say, 'Well, we didn't give birth to you, so you are now officially not ours'?"

It felt as though once again I was reliving my very first day in boarding school. First they shipped me off to boarding school, then they married me off, and now they disowned me. This time, my family was throwing me away permanently. How could they just throw me away as though I was a piece of garbage that could be left curbside? Again, I had no control over the situation. Talk about a loss of control, with every single panic setting in at the very same moment. I now belonged to no one and nothing. Make it or break it, I was on my own for the long haul.

I don't think anyone can even come close to understanding what it feels like to be disowned until you have experienced it. Can you imagine your father saying you are not his daughter and he wants nothing to do with you? Not entirely their fault, either—they could see me making a big mistake out of vulnerability and they did not want to see their daughter "suffer."

This one scenario took years to heal. The first year, I was so angry, there was no hope of healing. I said, "I will never forgive them for as long as I live." I just processed the event and reflected on what had happened. I simply could not comprehend why they would make such a drastic decision. To this day, I am still unable to comprehend the actual decision; however, I have gone through much self-forgiveness and forgiveness of them.

It was not easy. After the anger came the sadness of not belonging to anyone anymore, which of course compounded having been in boarding school. It was as though they had always been trying to hand me off to someone or somewhere throughout my life.

A few years after receiving the letter, I was finally in a place to heal at a deeper level and go through a process of forgiveness. I reached out to my friend Judy, who is a spiritual healer, to help me better understand my parents' decision to disown me as an adult. It was an eye-opening experience, indeed, in which she guided me mentally through a visualization to be in my father's place and to completely understand, if I were him, what would have made me make that very difficult decision. I concluded that he probably felt betrayed, given that he had dedicated his entire life to his family and now his daughter was doing something that he could not comprehend. Next came the processing of my mother's position. Healing involved the same process of stepping into her shoes and trying to understand the story through her lens. I concluded that she could not understand why I had made the decisions that I made. My parents had brought me up with the ideals of being courageous and standing up for what is right, and there I was, in her view, running away from life.

These healing sessions were the most emotional sessions I have ever done and yet the most gratifying. Without having gone through this phase of healing, I would not have been able to get to a place of self-forgiveness. Eight hours later, I was driving home, having cried and released huge amounts of anger, resentment, and guilt.

The sadness sometimes continues still, if a particular song comes on the radio, or I see someone my age with his or her parents. But it has become much easier to handle now, as I better understand why they did what they did, although it did not make the healing process any easier, that's for sure. This part of the costume still remains in the background, and sometimes it comes up for healing again, every so often. It's a patch that will forever remain in a hologram form, reminding me of the greatest test of all, forgiveness of self and others.

Critical Elements for Transitioning out of Your Costume

When I am coaching a client to take off his or her costume, the greatest emotional response I get is fear—fear of feeling exposed or vulnerable in front of other people. Also, a disconnect regarding "If I take the costume off, then who am I?" Clients often think when they remove the costume it means that they have to pretend as though the stories didn't happen. It's actually quite the contrary. Instead, you recognize and accept the stories, take the lesson from them, and move forward. You don't have to forget about yourself; you just don't allow the story to consume your mind. Remembering the difference between pain and suffering, don't linger in the story and think about it again and again. If you are consumed by your thoughts, how productive can you actually be in the workplace?

As a leader, do you want a team at your boardroom table that is looking at something from every angle and openly discussing all possibilities without hesitation about how they perceive what you're saying? Or would you rather work with a team that holds back on their thoughts simply because they are not equipped to say what really needs to be said? Once we start to understand the costumes that we all at some point wear, we gain a better acceptance of all views, because we may not know where the comment is coming from, but we can rest assured that there is a patch in that person's costume that may be stimulating the comment.

I believe that you can remove your costume and be the brilliant self that you are meant to be in complete freedom and liberation. Are you willing to risk taking the costume off, at all costs? Can you imagine the freedom and lightness you would feel by not defining yourself as one role or another? Can you just live in the moment and be what is needed for that moment?

If you have a desire to transition out of your costume, there are key critical elements to this process that I have discovered.

Acceptance

Accept that you are carrying around a costume woven of patches of your life experiences and that you have started to define yourself by these stories. For example, I once said to someone, "I don't have live plants in my house because I end up killing them and then feeling badly." Somewhere deep down I had told myself the story that I don't have a green thumb and plants just don't thrive around me. First, I had to accept the fact that I had told myself this story, which really had no basis at all, other than in the past some plants died due to one reason or another. Once I changed the story and really looked at why those plants died—such as because I was traveling a lot at the time and did not have time to take care of them—I came up with a very different perspective than labelling myself with "I don't have a green thumb."

At that time, I did not have a heart connection with plants either. In my perception they were more work added onto my day. Today, I have lots of thriving plants in my home because not only do I connect with them as a source of clarifying the air in my home, but also I have more time to nurture them and take care of them. So, I didn't all of a sudden over the years develop a green thumb. I had previously made myself believe a false story rather than look at the reality of what was going on in my life.

Some patches of our costume are very large and some are small. As you start to process the larger ones, the smaller ones will be very evident, as in my plants story.

Recognition

What I have learned after working in Change Management most of my career is that people do not change unless they experience something traumatic that makes them shift their life. My recognition that I was wearing a costume came from health issues, relationship issues, and financial issues. My life was falling apart fast and I needed to figure out why. This costume of trying to be someone for everyone else had become heavy, and the desire for freedom and liberation from it became stronger and stronger. It did not occur to me that I was organically changing slowly and my current life reality no longer served my journey going forward. My recognition that

I was wearing my life stories from my past meant that I would have to do something about them, and most of the time I was not willing to do something about them because I was a master justifier. I could justify anything in my current reality.

Clearing each patchwork in a costume takes time and patience, and I would get impatient with myself instead of just taking one story at a time and working through it. Now what happens, after doing so much of the work, is I can quickly recognize that it's a story I am telling myself, and the recognition alone neutralizes the story. That is the beautiful light at the end of the tunnel of self-discovery.

Willingness

You have to be willing to look at the entire story, not just at what you want to believe to be true. If you are not willing to look at the story from every angle, then you are not willing, plain and simple. Each story has many angles, and likely the one you are telling yourself is probably the one that justifies your own truth, the truth you want to be true.

I know that when I am willing to feel all the emotions tied to a story, I can literally walk through how every person in the story was probably feeling at the time.

We have to be willing to give people a fair chance and deeply understand their intentions rather than their actions. We have to be willing to have an open heart of curiosity. We have to be willing to consider we were wrong, and we have to be willing to say "I'm sorry," either to ourselves or to the others involved. This is not an easy step. It will take time, patience with yourself, and a willingness to heal through self-kindness and forgiveness.

Change the Story

Once you know you are willing and ready to revisit your truth of the story and consider all perspectives, it's time to shift how the story is for you. A story that might have started out as one of betrayal, resentment, and anger can become one of life's beautiful lessons. It might become one that has made you a better person due to the experience itself.

Carry forward the lesson the story has for you, rather than the story itself. This, again, is not an easy step, and you must go through the willingness step to really change the story, because it requires levels of forgiveness.

Surrender and Removal

Once you have identified the top ten stories in your patchwork, the real work begins, when you look at each story and shift each one to understand it from a different angle. Then the costume starts to come off, and the feelings of rawness, vulnerability, and exposure to the world as your true self become evident. I recommend spending a lot of alone time with yourself so that you don't put yourself into vulnerable places. Be in a safe place to feel exactly what you need to feel.

I called this my place of surrendering. My only other option was to continue living life the way I was living it, and that didn't seem like a viable option. So I surrendered to the emotions and to feeling crummy and like a victim. Yes, sometimes it's okay to just feel like a victim, the key being how fast you are able to move out of victimhood.

This surrender place is one without any worry and doubt about how you will be perceived or judged. This is where the true beauty resides. It is sometimes hiding the true authentic YOU in clear sight.

Chapter 9

Action Plan

Now that you have decided to surrender and are feeling like you want to move forward with this new you, let me create some action steps for you to have a great maintenance plan and never put on another costume. Each morning before you get out of bed, get into a ritual of asking yourself, "What story am I telling myself from yesterday that does not serve my soul journey going forward?" If you can't think of any, marvellous. That could mean that you are living in the moment and don't have any particular grudges from the day before. But if you are telling yourself a story that limits your soul journey, shift it! This question is part of my daily ritual. Sometimes stories will come out of nowhere from year ago, other times something really silly will come up, and other times nothing at all.

One day I woke up and asked myself this very question, "What am I carrying forward from yesterday?", and I recalled saying to someone the day before, "I am not really good with money." As I sat there on my bed, I then asked myself, "Where did that come from? Who says I am not good with money?"

As you can see, once you have done the work itself, then on a day-to-day basis you can catch these things much more quickly and easily.

Exercise—Removing the Quilt

1. Identify which story you want to work on. Pick one that may be easier to practice with first.
2. What are the key elements of the story? Who are the characters in the story? What factors do you believe to be true about yourself and others? When did this story take place? Where were you and under what circumstances did the story happen? When considering the elements of the story, I would recommend closing your eyes and trying to imagine what happened. Sometimes when our eyes are closed, we recall things that we may not otherwise remember.
3. What parts of the story do you repeat in your head the most?
4. What other facts are true about the story but you are choosing to ignore them?
5. What lessons have you learned from this story that you can carry forward?
6. What actions do you need to take to remove this story from your costume?
7. How does this story make you a better person today?

Chapter 10 Bringing It All Together through "Project Jivi"

Persian poet and Sufi Sultan Walad said, "Every human must be born twice: once from the womb of their mother and then again from his own body and his own existence."

Standing in the shower in January 2011, I knew in that moment that I had started the journey into being reborn from my own existence, and I would call this journey "Project Jivi." I committed to doing all the things that I had previously put on the back burner and ignored. This project would mean going to the depth of each part of my life with a support system of people who would surround me, guide me, and above all tell me exactly what I needed to hear, not bullshit me and tell what they might think I wanted to hear. I needed to hear the harsh truth that I had so eagerly and conveniently avoided. This project needed an action plan, and each day became another step toward ME. This project did not mean that I had to disappoint others and not help others. It just meant I made different choices that involved considering what *I* wanted and needed as well.

Once you make a commitment toward yourself, the Universe comes together and helps support that part of the journey for you by showing you signs of your next steps.

Pulling Together a Support Network

The next few months were filled with pulling together a support network of people I trusted. This included people to support my health, in particular getting to the bottom of my neuropathy; psychologically processing my divorce; learning from a financial coach; and practicing deep spiritual work to discover the lost person inside me. The right people simply started to emerge through personal connections—something was advertised on the radio, in a newspaper, or through a flyer I saw in a coffee shop. The commitment to make things better had led to the creation of a support system.

To be honest, I can't even explain how the right people just fall into place at the right time when you really desire to change, but I am living proof that it happens. For example, I was seeing a craniosacral therapist to guide me through my birth and the complications I was experiencing until recently due to my birth. I worked with him for about six months before I headed off to Sedona to work with others and experience the birthing cave. When I look back, the spiritual preparation was necessary before the physical experience of Sedona; working with the craniosacral therapist led me to complete the work in Sedona at the birthing cave.

My physical health recovery was the easiest to focus on in the beginning because it did not involve emotions; I was doing enough crying on my own. So, I began with daily walks at noon to get myself out of the house and by the ocean. I love the ocean, so it was easy. Then, once I started to get comfortable with walking every day, I saw an advertisement for something called TRX training. I learned TRX stood for Total Body Resistance Exercise. I was fascinated, because it offered to help me build physical strength. As I worked with my TRX trainer, his next-door neighbor had a sign on his car for yoga classes. That led to my attending my first yoga class.

The point I am trying to make here is that you just need to take the first step, and quite often that is what we fear the most.

Even as I write this, I realize there is something that I have always wanted to do, which is to teach children about the history of Sikhism. And yet, I am afraid to take the first step. "I don't have enough knowledge. They won't be interested in the topic. How will I prepare the lessons?" You get what I mean. I just need to take the first step.

As you can see, taking the first step can be a daily practice, not something you achieve and put a gold star of accomplishment beside. Every day we come across choices and decisions that call to us, and the bigger question is "Are you willing to listen and to take action?"

When it comes to putting together your health support network, it is important to be aware of what type of exercise your body responds well to, as well as what you enjoy doing. For the longest time, I was very hard on myself because I found myself not going to the gym and utilizing the membership, I could not follow through on my commitment to walk every day, and I didn't have the motivation to get out of bed for boot camp. For years, I felt that I was weak and not strong enough to do what I intended to do, and therefore I felt guilty and disappointed in myself.

Having neuropathy in my feet means I have constant nerve pain in both feet. Neuropathy limited my beliefs around exercise so that, for example, when I would go for a walk, I knew that when I came back home I would have increased pain that evening. Instead of looking for alternatives, I would not go for a walk and justify that to myself by saying, "I don't want to be in pain afterwards, so I will just not go."

Sometimes, we don't exercise or eat healthily because it's too time-consuming and the motivation is simply not there.

When I realized that there are options that I could explore, such as yoga or Chakradance, it opened up a new world for me. I could get healthy and have little or no impact on nerve pain. This motivated me to continue. When I first started to do yoga, I mentioned to my instructor that I would commit to coming for one year once a week. But in fact my only promise was that I would walk through her door, with no commitment to what would happen when I was in the room. Depending on how I was feeling with my pain level, we did what we could each week. Some days, I would just cry in her studio and she patiently listened. Other days I would do some yoga poses as my neuropathy allowed. And there have been days when I just lay on the floor on a yoga mat, talking about life with her. She did not judge me; she simply celebrated that I made it through her door each week.

When we put pressure on ourselves to be a certain way, there is more room for disappointment. I simply committed to walking through her door, and that is exactly what I did. Not pressuring yourself is the key here. Each day, see how you feel and what calls to you.

Some days, for me, it was yoga; some days, it was weight training; other days, I simply just went for a walk. I started to do things because they made me feel good, not because I was trying to lose weight. When we do things because they make us feel warm and tingly inside, our intention and motivation starts to shift.

At the same time, my life coach was helping me process what I wanted to do and what I wanted from life. I wanted, ignoring all fears, to have the courage to follow my heart's voice. As the stories that I knew to be true about myself started no longer to define who I am, I was left feeling "If I am not that, then what am I? Who am I?" In a sense, I was left feeling naked and exposed, because no longer could I wear a costume of those stories again. If you can imagine yourself standing at the busiest intersection you can think of with no clothes on, stark naked, and the world around you whizzing by in their own creative vortexes, you will know how I felt. In a weird way, I felt vulnerable and exposed and yet free and liberated in the same breath. I would often say to myself, "This is my rock bottom, so what am I worried about? It can't get any worse than being here. I am alone with no safety net to protect me."

Once you make the decision to remove the costume, then it's an ongoing series of beginnings that become easier and easier to heal each time. It's a gradual process that you commit to undertaking, no matter how long it takes you. I had an opportunity, an opportunity to redefine and rebuild who I was as I wanted to be, and I was ready to embark on a journey of self-discovery.

Building yourself from a place of nothingness is no easy task. It requires courage in yourself, faith in others, and a willingness to look at every single aspect of your life, while also realizing that each one is inseparable from the others. So, I spent the next year working on my physical, spiritual, and emotional health as a whole person in complete oneness. "Who do I want to be and what did I want to bring to the world?" My answer was not at all what I would have expected and brought me to a magical world that I had not anticipated.

Reconnecting Me with My Religion of Sikhism

My support system started reconnecting me with my religion of Sikhism, not from a religious perspective but more from a student perspective. If I were connecting with Sikhism from a religious perspective, its outward appearance, that would mean I would need to believe in not cutting my hair, not removing any hair at all, not eating meat, praying five times a day, waking up at four thirty in the morning, and so on. The list goes on and on. From a student perspective, I looked more at the essence and the foundation of Sikhism, which is more about how we live our lives, sharing what we earn with those less fortunate, meditating for the inner journey, only eating what we have earned with our own hands, and so on. So, I was interested in the essence of the actual foundation and not all the religious trappings. Sikhism is like a self-help manual for mankind. I can live the life of a Sikh by projecting Sikhism's values and foundation without being religious.

So, I wondered what these scriptures could teach me about why I was where I was in my life. I say reconnecting because I had grown up with an interest in all religions in general, as is encouraged in Sikhism. Being born into a Sikh family, I had been brought up in that environment. When I would listen to the words of the *Guru Granth Sahib* (the central scripture of Sikhism), I would find a peace inside my body that I could not explain and probably needed no explanation—it just was what it was. I would pray in the morning and evening for about four hours a day. Throughout the day, I would play Kirtan hymns in the background on my computer. From seven in the evening until bedtime was the most difficult time for me. It was when I missed my family and the kids post-divorce, so I would often do the evening prayers then.

During this time of reconnecting, I learned that every answer I seek external to myself is available internally—I need not search outside myself. I learned that staying in the moment is desirable because it is all that we actually have; we carry around our past and worry about our future unnecessarily. I also learned that we are the manifesters of our own destiny, and so it does not matter what my story was in the past. I have control of how my story will end. If I make different choices today, these choices plant seeds for the future, and my future is within what I can manifest.

Not everyone needs to go back to religion. It's more important to connect with the essence of something greater than yourself. Whether that is religion or meditation or even walking in the forest, accept whatever suits your wellbeing. Start to pay attention to what gives your heart joy, and do more of that each day.

You may be thinking, "How do I know what joy feels like for me?" Joy comes at those times when it feels as though your chest is going to explode with excitement. It comes at those times when you get teary-eyed with gratitude. It comes at those times when life feels well beyond love. As I went through my transition, the word "joy" had been missing from my vocabulary. Some of us spend so much time giving to other people that we rarely look at what gives us joy. It took me a while to even comprehend what joy looked like for me, yet I began to fill my days with joy. Small steps each day have brought me finally to the place of having days filled with joy. I have had to make sure I create time to enjoy something to fill my heart each day. What else could I even do with my time, with no husband, no kids, no family, and a very small handful of friends. So, I did simple things like having tea with a friend, reading a special book, listening to music, writing poems, volunteering at the soup kitchen, and sometime simply putting some lavender in the bathtub for a soak. Each one of these things brought some level of peace and joy to my heart.

Making the Right Things Happen

As a Type A personality, I went from always being on the go, doing multiple things at the same time, and sometimes attending up to three family functions in a weekend to having nothing to do, no one to be with, and no plans for my future. Two opposite sides of the pendulum. We often experience this when something impacts our health and wellbeing so that we have to seclude ourselves to figure things out. My desire would be that we all accept this seclusion as a normal part of rediscovering ourselves and that we learn sooner that we need time out from life to take care of ourselves now rather than later. Unfortunately, many of us miss the signs that we are given and we continue until we crash.

My health needed a major overhaul, as you can imagine, so once I was walking each day, I started to see a chiropractor, an Ayurvedic practitioner, a massage therapist, a life coach, and a craniosacral therapist.

Now, you may think doing all these activities cost a lot of money, and yes, they did. However, are you worth it? That is the bigger question. At this point in my life, I knew I was worth it. I made it happen by reducing costs in other areas so that I would not jeopardize myself.

When we truly want something, we make it happen. That's just reality. Think about a time in your life when you wanted something so badly you would do anything to get it. Maybe it was new boots or jeans. Maybe it was a piece of jewelry or furniture. We are happy saving money for material things, and yet when it comes to our own health and wellbeing, there is always something else that takes precedence.

Remember, "Project Jivi" required me to think about myself first; getting myself better was my goal. I would sacrifice other things that I probably did not need anyway. Around Christmas 2010, I remember a friend asking me for some financial support to give to a women's shelter, as they needed to buy some winter clothes. It would be an investment of a hundred dollars—a hundred dollars that I could not spare, as I was using eighty dollars on my monthly massage therapy sessions. I told my friend, whom I really wanted to help, that I could only spare twenty dollars each month from my massage therapy money. She paid the cost up front and I would pay her back twenty dollars each month. I had only made my first payment to her when, much to my surprise, my massage therapist said, "This session is on me because you have been coming here for over six months"! Remember at the beginning of this chapter, I said that once you commit, the Universe will come together to make it happen? Well, the Universe just made that happen.

Over the course of the next few years, an unlimited number of examples of manifestations occurred. I would make a commitment to something and patiently wait. Without skipping a beat, there it would be, in some way, shape, or form: the exact thing I had committed to would happen. Sometimes I had to be more patient, as apparently my timing is not always the same as Divine timing.

Putting yourself first feels strange in the beginning. However, it's important to remember you are putting yourself first not in a selfish way but rather in a way that respects your self-care boundaries. "Project Jivi" became more and more clear as each day passed. There were high emotions at certain times of the day, and other times went by super fast. The project continued as I reconnected with myself each day, putting one foot in front of the other and sometimes even sideways to move forward. Each person played a pivotal role for a specific moment in time. I continued with some aspects of my support system throughout the year; others came and went. Sometimes I would be in Chakradance and other months I would try something else like weight training. Sometimes I would go back to praying and other days I would meditate or journal. Some days I would want to go out and be around people and other days I would want to be by myself. All I had to do was listen to what my heart wanted to do and then do it.

I had such a difficult time most of my life putting closure to things, especially with relationships. So, I had to learn to put myself ahead and respect my own self-care program. The two groups of people who were consistent in my journey of self-discovery were my friends and certain family members, such as my children and my sister. My spiritual mentor, coach, friend, and "Soul Caretaker," as I refer to her, was and still is the most significant pillar in my journey. She was and always is there, gently and quietly guiding me through "*in*lightening" conversations (Ruby Bedi calls them "*in*lightening" conversations because it's all about the inward journey), recommending prayers or meditations, helping me forgive and move forward each day, and most significantly, helping me be real with all the things that I need to process. By "be real," I mean looking at things from all angles and not just the angles that serve my ego.

To this day, she continues to be a guiding light for my path—just enough for me to see through the darkness, and then she lets me figure out the way. A great spiritual mentor will not give the answers as much as we sometimes might wish. Rather, they light the way just enough for us to guide ourselves. She is the same person who called that day when I stood on the balcony considering ending my life. She is the same person who called when my health fell apart. And she is the same person who calls me every now and again when the light inside me starts to diminish even slightly.

Find your soul fuel igniter and hang on to them for dear life. That person is your greatest cheerleader, bullshit mirror, ego controller, and your friend.

Core Values

As a part of my role as an Organizational Development Consultant, I have facilitated hundreds of meetings helping organizations define their core values.

As a part of my own support during my work of coming home to my authentic self, I really questioned the values, ethics, and morals that I had held on to so strongly over many years. It was as though I was carrying a backpack filled with weights, and each weight was labeled with words like "respect," "integrity," "trust," and "honesty." You know, all the words we carry around, thinking that's who we are and what we reflect.

In the workplace, as a part of strategic planning, we are trained to develop core values that are important to the team and the organization. Throughout my career, I can count on one hand organizations that truly walk the talk of these core values and can give examples of behavior that depict them playing out in those organizations.

Don't get me wrong. I am not saying an organization shouldn't have core values. But if it does, each and every person in the organization should know them and be able to give examples of their own behaviors that depict them. Think about that for a moment. Why is it necessary to have a respectful workplace policy? Many of the organizations that I have worked with as a consultant have had the highest number of respect-related issues and grievances. Doesn't that tell us that what we are doing is not working? Having a policy in place does not help create a respectful workplace. As a matter of fact, it provides a document by which we can judge each other.

What if, instead, each person were dedicated to respecting themselves and others through tools and techniques that they could use? Here is the angle to consider. We still carry these values around because we may not yet have been tested in them. For example, if I thought my child were so sick I needed to take her to a doctor and buy her medication and I had no money, would I steal medicine for her? The answer was simple: yes, I would. So, where did my value of honesty and integrity go? Was I holding onto these values to use when convenient? Did I even known if I would uphold them in reality? Was it possible to release my heavy backpack and just be who I could be in each moment in time?

The freedom we gain by making moment-to-moment decisions about our values, ethics, and morals completely changes the heaviness some of us feel in upholding all the things we carry around in our backpack.

Project YOU

Project YOU (insert your name in place of "YOU") is about telling yourself and the world that you respect and love yourself enough to work on yourself first. Think about it for a moment. What if each one of us around the world only ever worked on ourself? Would the world not be a better place?

The support system you create around yourself is absolutely critical in redefining who you are in each element of your life. These things are not easy to do by yourself. You need a support system, and your support system also continues to change as you grow organically yourself. A yoga teacher who is great for today may not be the one you continue with. A spiritual teacher who serves your needs today may not be the one who continues to meet your needs your entire life. Your current counselor or

Chapter 10

coach may not be the most effective for you as you continue to grow. When you outgrow something or someone, learn to recognize that and move on.

This project introduces you to the self-discovery process of "Who am I?" No one can walk this path for you, as much as I might want to. However, people can walk with you, in support of you, encouraging you, inspiring you, and reminding you that your true, authentic self will be worth all the emotions that arise.

Whether you are a CEO, a leader of your department, or a team member reading this book, it's important to remember that no longer do people show up at work having left their problems behind. What we are dealing with at home manifests in the workplace in various forms.

Earlier I wrote that the answers to "Who am I?" and "What am I here to do?" were not what I expected. So, here is what I have learned. We cannot define who we are, because we are dynamic and we keep shifting. You can only be who and what you are in each given moment. You can only serve from your purpose in each given moment. So how can you come up with something that is a defining statement? It is just impossible.

In one moment I am a mother, and in another moment I am a worker, and in another moment a daughter, and below everything, I am myself. This journey of self-discovery must be walked alone. Don't let anyone tell you they can heal you. They can only create an environment that is safe for you, an environment in which you can heal yourself, based on your own readiness. The right people to support you will know what platform you are on for healing yourself.

Following My Dreams

When I was faced with leaving my job in 2015, I thought the only pathway was to find another job in healthcare and do what I know best and am most comfortable with. That would give me a predictable income. I was a single mom with two kids in university. It was insane to think anything else was even possible.

I remember sitting and staring at my computer, thinking, "Can I practice what I preach to others? Is there another solution that may be different but has advantages of its own?"

I brainstormed many things and I concluded that I could use my Registered Retirement Savings Plan money to follow my dreams now rather than waiting until my retirement. I would need to make some financial adjustments, such as being on a strict budget, reaching out for financial support, working on a financial plan with my ex-husband for our children's university costs, etc.

Anything is possible if and when we have the innate desire to manifest it, and I am living proof that anything is possible.

Where did this mindset come from, that there is no pathway other than the conventional and traditional finding of a job to fund our life? As I processed this mindset, I realized it came from my childhood feeling that I had no control over my life's decisions or choices.

We go through life conforming to what others think success is for us, a pseudo-being who may be miserable at heart and yet can put on a very good show for the public and live the life others intend for us rather than what we intend for ourselves. Rather than take accountability and recognize we are living a life for others, we choose to harvest anger and resentment that manifest in the work environment.

Chapter 10

A team member once told me the biggest gift I could give her was making her recognize that she was in control of her life choices. How profound, that we need to realize this when it should be innately who we are, accountable for our life right now. Somewhere we lose the ability to even think we are in control. So, coming back to the destiny pen, your pen has the ability to change your life to exactly what you want it to be.

Screwed Up Sense of Success

I had come to believe that work was exactly that—work. It was not meant to be fun; rather, it was something you did to get a paycheck and provide for your family. Each time early in my career I had come home and complained about some thing or another that happened at work, I would hear, "It's work, Jivi. If it were meant to be joyous, it would not be called 'work.' " Somewhere along the way, not only did I begin to believe that was true, but I did a beautiful job at justifying being miserable, stressed out, and overwhelmed at work, thinking that meant I was successful.

This very screwed-up sense of success became as clear as water one day a month after leaving my job, when I sat on my deck sipping tea. I received a phone call from a past leader who said, "So. What are you up to?"

For a moment, I felt the urge to lie and say I was doing something of utmost importance. Many excuses ran through my head at lightning speed, such as I was emailing, doing my business plan, preparing for some marketing, looking for a job. All these in a matter of seconds, because I didn't know how I could say, "Sitting on my deck having tea and doing nothing." What would he think about me as a person? Would he think I was not being productive and would therefore pass judgment on my credibility?

Now, you are probably intrigued by what I actually did say.

I gathered some courage and said, "I'm sitting on my deck, enjoying some tea and watching the ocean."

"Phew," I thought. "I said it."

There was an awkward pause, and his response hit me like a ton of bricks. "Man, I wish I could be there with you right now. Life is good to you!"

I wanted to respond by saying, "But you have the choice to make your life this way. You just have to make different choices. I have made choices that allow me to sit on the deck at certain times of the day and have tea." Why is it that we as humans think that this perception of the good life only happens to certain people? Miserable home and work environments are that way because we choose to stay in them and not do something about them. We don't do something about them because we anticipate that the pain of changing our current reality is so big that we won't be able to deal with the consequences.

Muderella Became My Goal

Last year in January 2015, I decided to do Muderella in July that year. Muderella is a twenty-three-obstacle course walk and run for cancer held in Whistler, British Columbia. July was far enough away that if I wanted to back out, I thought I could. Over the next few months I worked with my trainer to get myself into the best shape possible, not just to complete the obstacle course itself, but also to gain some muscle strength. I had imagined the race to be well beyond my physical capability, and yet I had this innate desire to take on the challenge, while not really fully understanding what it would take to complete it. The neuropathy I have in my hands and feet not only makes them numb but sends out random pain signals.

What I remember the most about training was every time I

Chapter 10

would say, "There is no way I am going to do this," my trainer would smile gently and say, "Jivi, I am going to be there with you every step of the way. I will pull you through each exercise, and at the end you can trust that I will be standing right there to pull you out of the water."

In the last few weeks, she would remind me, "You are ready and you will do it, even if I have to drag you through the course myself!" I can honestly say to this day, she stood by her word. Whenever I wanted to give up, she dragged me—not in the literal sense, of course, but more from the perspective of "You're not going to give up, Jivi. You've got this, Jivi. You can do it, I know you can."

I trained with her over the six months, and before I could consider backing out, July was on us and we were on our way to Whistler. I remember wondering as we drove there, "What was I thinking? I am never going to be able to do this. I am crazy." Many other gremlins were shouting from their perches on my shoulders, telling me exactly how I was going to fail. I had not only prepared physically but I had gone through each obstacle in the course online multiple times to mentally prepare myself about how the obstacle was set up, what people said the year before about each actual obstacle, and what feedback there was online about the challenges people had in any particular obstacle.

I had already decided which obstacles I would not do because I was claustrophobic, I did not know how to swim, and above all, I probably would not make it through the second obstacle. I embraced each word the gremlins were saying and then thought, "I am going to do this anyway. What's the worst thing that can happen?"

As I approached the starting line with my team members, boy, was I in for a surprise! I was staring up at a five-and-a-half-mile mountain trail that would take us to the obstacles. No one had told me there was an uphill trek before we even got to the obstacles!

"No way, no way at all am I doing this. This is crazy!"

As I bickered and complained and probably said some unpleasant words toward my trainer, I slowly walked one foot in front of the other, while my team (put together by our team leaders) one-by-one supported and encouraged me to keep going. There was a huge life lesson there in each step. In much the same way that we have a vision for ourselves and it is necessary to take one step at a time toward that vision, I focused on just each step up that trail. As I watched my feet move that day, I realized each step took me a little further to the completion of my goal. This team encouraged, inspired, and motivated me to prove to myself that I was not my illness, nor did it control me.

When we arrive at the first obstacle, I was already tired, exhausted, mad, angry, and resentful. As I looked at the obstacle, it seemed fairly easy. It required balancing not too far off the ground. All was okay with the world again for now. We then arrived at the obstacle I had prepared to not do. It was a black tube you had to wiggle your way down into muddy water. "Nope. I am not getting into a dark tube inches away from my face. What if I get stuck?"

As I stood there contemplating whether or not to get into the black tube, I wondered two things: "Can I rise above my fear and prove to myself I can do anything, or should I avoid doing this obstacle knowing full well I will regret avoiding it later." As I stood there watching my team go through the tunnel one by one, a woman from another team who was standing behind me said, "Go on. If you get stuck, I'll push you out."

On the far side, my team was waiting to pull me out of the

Chapter 10

water. "I am going in. This is it," I thought. "Here I go." And before I knew it, my team leader had my hand and was pulling me out of the muddy water. "Phew, what an accomplishment!" I thought, "much like in life, when we accomplish something and then have a vitalizing and encouraging feeling to do more."

As I stared up the next hill that we had to climb, I quickly fell back into my complaining of "There is no way." My team encouraged me to take the next step, one step at a time.

There were many lessons along the rest of the course, which I won't share in detail. But I will say that the day would not have been possible without my team leaders, my team members, and a gentleman who was a friend of one our team leaders, a man I refer to as "my Angel." He showed up that day just when I needed someone to hold my hand and guide me each step of the way. I don't think even he realized how pivotal his role was, not just on that course but also in my life journey itself. That day I learned from him two very important things—you don't know your own potential unless you have pushed yourself beyond what you think is ever possible and someone gives you their hand to help. There is no ego in allowing them to help you through a tough space. I learned that when you have the right support in your life, there is absolutely nothing you can't accomplish.

Now I must walk you through the end of the obstacle course, because many of the greatest milestones of my life occurred there. As I completed the second-to-last obstacle, I was physically, emotionally, spiritually done. I was toast. There was nothing left in me at that point with which to even cry. As I stared at the hill that went uphill toward the last obstacle, I fell on the grass staring at my Angel. I said, "No way. There is no way. I need to just lie down here and sleep. There is no way I will do this."

My Angel said, "It's okay to rest for a bit. But you will do this because you have come so far. I will not let you quit now."

So, I rested for a bit and came to realize he was not joking. He was waiting for me to get back up. Reluctantly, I stood up on legs that were now jelly from exertion and frozen from cold water. "Come on, legs, let's do this," I thought. "Just one more obstacle and then I am done!"

The last obstacle was to climb up a fisherman's net to get to the top of some slides and then slide down into five feet of cold, muddy water. After a long day, that might even sound like fun to some people. Did I forget to mention that I do not swim and am scared of the water?

I made it to the top of the slide and, as I sat there, I looked over at the volunteer who was helping people go down the slide and said, "Please help me off this thing. I am not doing this." His response was not what I wanted to hear: "I am going to come over there and kiss you on the cheek. Then you are going to let go."

I looked at him in utter disbelief and, before I knew it, he was sitting beside me, kissing me on the cheek, and saying, "It's time to let go." A complete stranger, again, not even knowing the extent of what he had just inspired in me.

As I let go, I felt the beauty of surrendering and the feeling of freedom that comes with it. As promised, there was my trainer and team to pull me out of the water. As I came out, not comprehending what anyone was saying to me, I realized I would never be the same person, ever.

Lessons from Muderella

Many people have asked me what I learned overall. They have asked specifics, such as what it was like being submerged in water without knowing what was going to happen. When I was in the water, I felt the duality of life and death in the same moment. It felt as though I was in my mother's womb and yet at the very same time I felt like I had died. It was a beautiful experience of the duality in which we live our lives all the time. Living life to come alive and yet knowing we are inevitably going to die one day. I remember seeing a glimpse of the sunlight through the water and reaching out my fingers, trusting that my team would keep me safe. I remember my team leader taking my hand and pulling me out of the water. Before I knew it, I sat with blankets around me to give me some warmth.

When my daughter came to pick me up, I had gone into hypothermia. I saw how proud she was of me as she helped me get into a warm bath to return my body to its normal temperature. I realized in that moment how precious is each person in our life. I realized how much I love my kids and how much I want them to know that anything is possible.

There are many more lessons from this one experience that relate directly to our work environments, such as sometimes the monsters in our head are much bigger than reality itself. We each need a team we can trust and count on to help us through something that we don't think we can do. We have to be honest with our leader about what we fear the worst, so we are better supported. Obstacles move us forward into more encouragement to do the next task. Above all, this experience taught me that my health issues are not my limitations. They do not define who I am and what I can or cannot do. I cannot be shackled by my own limiting beliefs.

As I stood there in hypothermic shock in the hotel room with my daughter, she slowly helped me undress and get into the hot shower. She kept saying, "Mom, I am so proud of you."

All I kept thinking was, "I did it. I actually did it." And it felt like there is absolutely nothing that I cannot accomplish. I looked into my daughter's eyes, sobbing, and said, "Oh, my God, I just completed Muderella!"

Letting go of the costume has not just been about shedding the emotional stories but also about shedding the physical and mental limitations I had placed on myself. I had to push beyond those limitations to really live the life I desired. I had to believe that anything was possible, but I had to desire it and want it strongly enough. You are the creator of your life, and as long as you are willing to accept that your life today is exactly what you have made it to be through your sequence of choices, then you can make different choices today to have a magnificent you tomorrow.

Exercise—Identifying Your Support Team

When you are putting together your support team to help you remove your costume, there are some key factors to keep in mind. Ask yourself the questions below and then find the top three people per category who can help support your journey. Identify people whom you trust, can be vulnerable with, and don't feel any judgement from, as you need to be very comfortable being raw and exposed with them. If there is only one person you can think of, then just use one person in that category.

～

What do I need to do to keep me the most grounded and centered?

Who are the top three people who can help support me with this?

Where can I build creativity in my life?

Who are the top three people who can help support me with this?

Who can help me gain self-worth and power within myself?

Who are the top three people who can help support me with this?

Who or what can support my self-love development?

Who are the top three people who can help support me with this?

Who/What can help me find my authentic voice?

Who are the top three people who can help support me with this?

Who can help me enhance my intuition?

Who are the top three people who can help support me with this?

Who can help me discover my soul script?

Who are the top three people who can help support me with this?

Epilogue

The current reality of your life is all about the choices you have made; you and only you are responsible for your current reality. For a new tomorrow, we must make different choices today.

Stating affirmations is a beautiful way of reminding ourselves to make different choices so that we create a future that is aligned in heart and soul. Here are some affirmations that I have used over the last few years to remind myself continually of how I can be the master of my own destiny. You can say them aloud to yourself, write them on sticky notes to place around your house, or even record yourself saying them in your phone and listen to them when you feel any emptiness in your heart.

Today, I choose to look at life with the eye of magnificence within the simple pleasures of my reality.

Today, I choose to make the decisions that feel good to my gut and are stepping-stones toward a larger life script.

Today, I choose to not stay in relationships just because I am afraid of the pain of letting go.

Today, I choose to be my authentic self so that I never leave something unsaid or a voice unheard.

Today, I choose to not wear a costume anymore so as to not carry around weight that I do not need.

Today, I choose to love others and myself freely and openly without worry of being hurt.

Today, I choose to forgive others and myself as I am simply passing by this world for a short period of time.

Today, I choose to keep my perspective when things may seem to go wrong, and remember that this too shall pass and become a life lesson.

And today, I choose to live reminding myself that one day I will no longer be here and for that reason, each moment I will live to come alive in my Divinity.

As we all continue to peel away the layers of healing within new situations that arise or old memories that are ready to be released, it only gets easier. I have walked the hero's journey as many of you have or may be on right now, each of us returning with a magnificent elixir for making the world a better place. I have returned for now as a teacher with my elixir, one of helping others as they travel their own hero's journey through the process of self-inquiry, self-realization, and self-actualization. What I bring to you is assistance in inspiring within you courage in your darkest hour, strength when you think you cannot continue anymore, and love in its purest form without any judgment. Helping you explore your soul script is the divine gift I share with you. Your journey will be yours and you will come out of it with your own elixir and teachings that you may desire to share with the world.

Chapter 10

Through this story of my life's challenges, I show you that there is a beautiful magnificence that can transpire from our life events. I exemplify that you can turn any situation around to see that without that life situation you would not be who you are today. Each situation that occurs in your life is divinely guided for that exact moment in time so that you become exactly the person you are today. If any of the scenarios had not occurred in my life in their exact sequence, I would not be who I am today. Each event that has happened in your life has happened for you and only you. You are the only magnificent being amongst seven billion other with your exact genetic makeup, your life experiences, your education, your triggers and "baggage," and your life lessons. It's time to claim your brilliance and decide how you will share your magnificence with the world.

Author Biography

Jivi Saran knows from experience that mindfulness in the workplace results in powerful relationships, productivity, creativity, and focus. Many teams resist this methodology so Jivi uses her keen Corporate Mentalist skills, observing behavior and thought patterns in team participants to shift their openness in giving themselves and their team members permission to show up at work wholly and completely. As a leader of a six-year experiment testing the concept, Jivi observed firsthand the power of this practice and has the data to prove it. Jivi now travels the world helping teams become more powerful, creative, and focused producing low-to-no turnover rates, incomparable efficiency, and healthy team members in all areas of their lives.

About Jivi

If you are an organizational leader that would like to be cutting edge in your approach to leadership and team excellence

OR

If you are an individual ready to remove the heaviness of your costume and would like to work with someone who knows exactly how it feels to walk the Hero's Journey,

1. Here are the most pleasurable ways to work with Jivi

    a. The Corporate Soul- Your immortal Legacy
    b. Unveiling the True You-The Hero's Journey
    c. Permission to be you-The Good, Bad, Best of showing up to work
    d. Organizational Mindfulness Demystified
    e. Making the impossibility of happier workplaces, possible

6. Business Consulting – Leadership and Team Excellence (The Corporate Soul Program)

7. Leadership and Team- Workshops and Retreats

8. Online Individual Coaching

9. Online Mindfulness Program

If you have been touched by anything that you have read in this book, I would love to hear from you, take the first step and just give me a call or send me an email.

Email - jcheema@windsofchange.ca
Website - www.thecorporatementalist.ca
Facebook Page - www.facebook.com/thecorporatementalist/
Contact - 250 714 6129